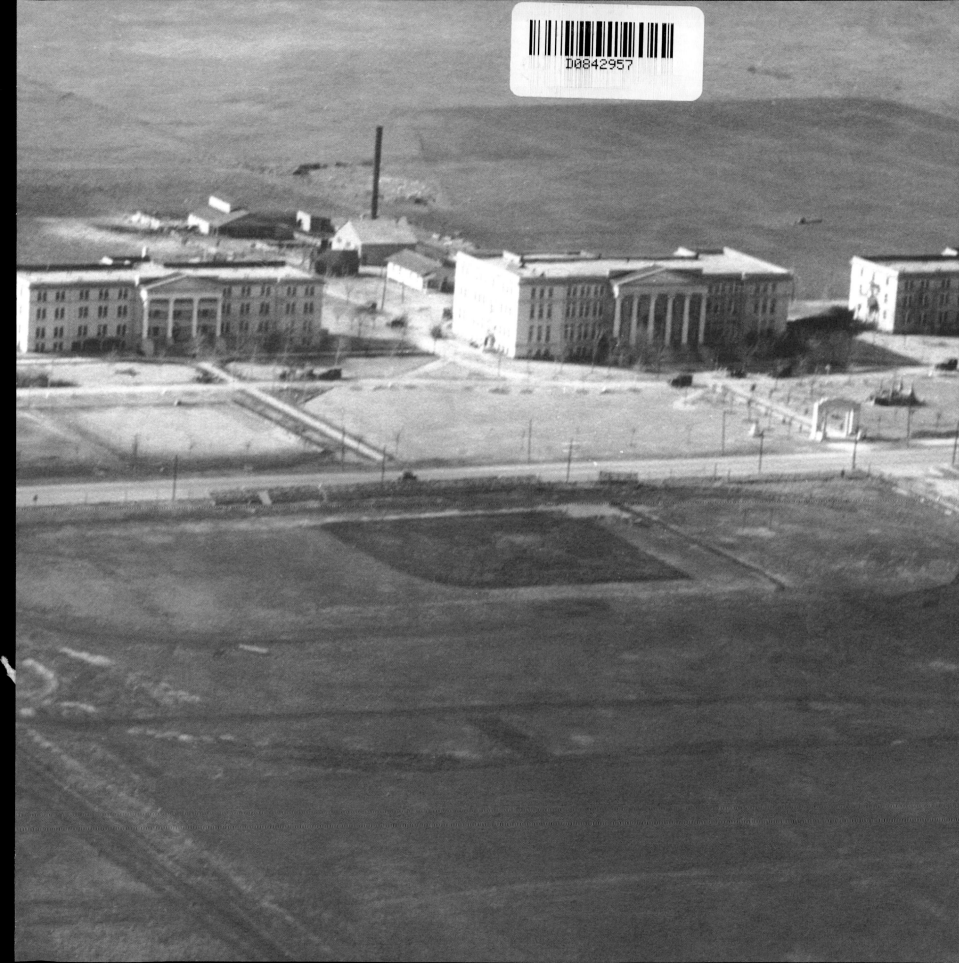
D0842957

A CENTURY
of PARTNERSHIP
FORT WORTH AND TCU

A CENTURY *of* PARTNERSHIP

FORT WORTH AND TCU

EDITED BY MARY L. VOLCANSEK

A Joint Project of The
Center for Texas Studies at TCU
and TCU Press, Fort Worth, Texas

CENTURY OF PARTNERSHIP — CELEBRATING TCU IN FORT WORTH

Compilation copyright © 2011 The Center for Texas Studies
Photographs copyright © 2011 TCU
TCU and Fort Worth: Our Success Is Your Success copyright © 2011 by Mary L. Volcansek
Closing the Circle: TCU from Fort Worth to Fort Worth copyright © 2011 by Gene Allen Smith
Impressions of Academics at TCU During the Last 100 Years copyright © 2011 by Bob J. Frye
TCU, Fort Worth, and the Arts copyright © 2011 by Ron Tyler
Fort Worth and TCU's Campus Life copyright © 2011 by Vicki Vinson Cantwell
The TCU Campus: Then and Now copyright © 2011 by Mike Mullins
One Hundred Years of TCU Athletics copyright © 2011 by Mark Mourer

Library of Congress Cataloging-in-Publication Data

A century of partnership : Fort Worth and TCU / edited by Mary L. Volcansek.
    p. cm.
  Includes index.
"A Joint Project of The Center for Texas Studies at TCU and TCU Press."
  ISBN 978-0-87565-417-1 (cloth : alk. paper)
  1. Texas Christian University--History. 2. Fort Worth (Tex.)--History. 3. Community and college--Texas--Fort Worth--History. I. Volcansek, Mary L., 1948-
  LD5311.T382C46 2011
  378.764'5315--dc22
                              2010023249
TCU Press
P. O. Box 298300
Fort Worth, Texas 76129
817.257.7822
http://www.prs.tcu.edu
To order books: 800.826.8911

Designed by fusion29, Fort Worth, Texas
Printed and bound in China by Everbest through Four Colour Imports, Ltd., Louisville, Kentucky

Composed in Sabon, designed by Jan Tschichold in 1967 and
Neutraface, designed by Christian Schwartz in 2002

CONTENTS

FOREWORD

The partnership between Texas Christian University and Fort Worth is 100 years strong and growing stronger.

In 2010, Texas Christian University celebrated a Century of Partnership—its 100th year in Fort Worth—and the growth both the university and this city have seen in that short century is amazing.

One hundred years ago, a fire at its campus in Waco left TCU looking for a new home. Thankfully, it found one here in Fort Worth. TCU had humble beginnings after it came to Fort Worth—with only a handful of modest buildings and grounds near the Tarrant County Courthouse. Since then, however, the university has grown, improved, and earned a reputation that reaches far beyond this region.

That has made TCU an integral part of the fabric of Fort Worth.

Helping nurture that growth was the support of many of the community leaders in Fort Worth. In 1923, Mary Couts Burnett created a trust that not only built the library that bears her name, but also helped the university survive the financial challenges of the Great Depression. Amon G. Carter led the campaign to raise funds to build a football stadium in 1929, and in the 1940s a group of Fort Worth businessmen raised $5.5 million to build or renovate sixteen buildings on campus.

That community support has helped the university grow, and TCU has helped our city grow.

Fort Worth, 100 years ago, was a little town—a mere 73,000 lived here. Today, nearly ten times that number live here. This great city has transitioned from a rough-and-tumble frontier town to a place where cowboy heritage melds seamlessly with refined culture, producing a "big little-town" feel that is home to a diverse population.

TCU has played a vital role in the evolution of Fort Worth.

It is a common bond that has blossomed for 100 years—which sounds like a long time, but in a world that is eons old, it is a mere blink of an eye. For all the great things that have happened, they are merely the first steps in what promises to be a long-standing march forward for both the university and this city.

TCU and Fort Worth share a rich history of working today to create a better tomorrow, of turning obstacles into opportunity, of rejecting the way things are so that we can make things the way they should be—for the next 100 years, and beyond.

– Michael J. Moncrief
Mayor, City of Fort Worth

1

TCU AND FORT WORTH:
OUR SUCCESS IS YOUR SUCCESS

MARY L. VOLCANSEK

Yearbook 1990, page 112. Recreation and Travel section of yearbook.

The year 2010 began with Fort Worth's going purple—literally. Fort Worth Mayor Mike Moncrief and TCU Chancellor Victor Boschini even attempted to dye the Trinity River purple. Although the river refused to cooperate, the city and the university celebrated a partnership, a happily, profitably symbiotic relationship, as they had for a century. TCU's perfect 12-0 football season, its Mountain West Conference title, and its first ever Bowl Championship Series (BCS) appearance did not lead to a victory in the 2010 Tostitos Fiesta Bowl. Nonetheless, the enthusiasm that TCU and Fort Worth share for each other's successes continues, as it has since the university moved to "where the West begins" with the signing of a contract between TCU and Fairmount Land Company on May 10, 1910.

Fort Worth and TCU formed an ideal partnership in part because the two share a number of common roots. Although Fort Worth originated as a military establishment in 1849, it was incorporated as a city by the Texas State Legislature in 1873, the same year that Addison and Randolph Clark opened AddRan College for Men and Women in Thorp Spring. Only the courageous would have chosen locations distant from military protection and vestiges of civilization. That frontier spirit and can-do attitude that imbued the founders both of TCU and of Fort Worth have prevailed over the years, enabling each to pursue excellence.

Town and gown often clash when faculty and students from elsewhere attempt to place their stamp on their host city or when a municipality views a university as a hindrance to its political goals. TCU and Fort Worth avoided that potential pitfall largely through goodwill and solid leadership on both sides. Fort Worth embraced the idea that every world-class city needs a world-class university and steadily supported TCU's progress in that direction. TCU recognized that the city offered an excellent recruiting tool for luring the best faculty and student talent to the university, to create a learning environment for students in the arts, social sciences, business, engineering, energy studies, humanities, science and healthcare, education, and ranch management.

By the fiftieth anniversary of TCU's move to Fort Worth in October of 1960, the city's population had grown from 73,000 to 353,000, and the university's enrollment had exponentially expanded from 362 to 8,381. Both the *Fort Worth Star-Telegram* and the *Fort Worth Press* carried special sections commemorating fifty years of successful partnership, and the university hosted a series of events on campus to thank the city. Fort Worth's City Council passed a resolution concluding that:

> From 1910, *when the City of Fort Worth first donated land for the Texas Christian University campus to the present, University and City have worked in close harmony in building a great Fort Worth. Such cooperation will continue as Texas Christian University and the City of Fort Worth gird to meet the challenge of service that the next fifty years will bring.*

The reciprocal nature of TCU's and Fort Worth's mutually beneficial partnership was evident from the beginning. In 1921, Dean E.R. Cockrell, the first chair of TCU's Department of Law, asked for leave from the university to run for mayor of Fort Worth. Even though he resigned before the end of his term to assume the presidency of a college in Missouri, he first succeeded in establishing a city-manager form of government in Fort Worth. That governmental arrangement, somewhat novel in 1921, continues into the twenty-first century.

Whereas talent from TCU's faculty and staff has benefited the city, the Fort Worth community has also supported TCU, particularly financially, since its founding. In 1923, Mary Couts Burnett created a trust that not only built the university library that bears her name, but also helped TCU survive the financial exigencies of the Great Depression. Fort Worth's greatest booster, Amon G. Carter, led a campaign to raise funds to build a football stadium in 1929. Similarly, Ed Landreth single-handedly raised 80 percent of the total goal for the Diamond Jubilee Building Fund Campaign between 1941 and 1946. During that same time, a group of Fort Worth businesspeople known as the Building Program Committee raised $5.5 million to build or renovate sixteen buildings on the TCU campus.

Other Fort Worth institutions enabled TCU to find outlets for its talents. Between 1938 and 1941, TCU radio students were able to air more than one hundred fifty programs on commercial radio stations KTAT and WBAP. Now, KTCU offers students a broadcast experience and adds one more option on the FM dial for Fort Worth listeners. In 1948, the university reciprocated the city's hospitality by staging a rodeo and downtown parade. In 1961, TCU became the host for the Van Cliburn International Piano Competition and, although the venue for the competition has moved, the university remains involved in its activities. The city continues to serve as a laboratory for TCU students, with internships and service learning projects in schools, engineering firms, courts and other government offices, hospitals,

Yearbook 1995, page 7.
TCU spirit.

clinics, and businesses. TCU also offers the city two experimental schools, Starpoint and Kinder-Frogs, for children with special learning needs, and the Miller Speech and Hearing Clinic provides outstanding services to citizens of the city. TCU offers a wide range of music, theater, dance, and art to the city's already rich artistic environment.

TCU has also offered first-class National Collegiate Athletic Association (NCAA) Division 1A athletic competition to the city. Football, basketball, baseball, and a number of individual sports for both men and women. Even though TCU has not won a national championship in football since 1938, it has offered Division 1A athletics to residents of Fort Worth. The TCU golf team can practice on the finest courses, many of them belonging to private country clubs. The women's equestrian team benefits from the largesse of Fort Worth citizens. Even in these non-academic endeavors, both the city and the university share victories and defeats.

The presence of the university in Fort Worth served to grease the economic wheels of the growing metropolis, and many students, faculty, and

Yearbook 1986, page 4. Members of Sigma Chi fraternity ride proudly down University Drive pulling their float in the Homecoming Parade.

staff who came to TCU remained in Fort Worth thereafter, charmed by the city's sense of place, its history, its future, and its friendliness. Not surprisingly, therefore, the city was willing to work with TCU to help the university achieve its dreams. One of those was expansion of the campus in the early 1960s. At that time TCU covered 138 acres, but the administration wanted to acquire the 106 additional acres that constituted the city-owned Worth Hills Golf Course. The City Council approved sale of the land to TCU, and city voters ratified the action in 1961.

That welcoming atmosphere persists, as I learned quickly when I arrived on campus in the summer of 2000 to assume the deanship of the new AddRan College of Humanities and Social Sciences. I, along with fellow new deans Sam Deitz of the school of education, Bob Lusch of the school of business, and Scott Sullivan of the school of fine arts, began trying to meet leaders in the city. Not being fond of cold calls, I assigned my administrative assistant, Sharon Campbell, the task of calling a lengthy list of local luminaries to schedule appointments. I would overhear Sharon calling, identifying me, spelling my name, and explaining patiently, "it's pronounced 'Volcansick,' like a sick volcano." Not one person turned her down for an appointment, not because of me, but

Yearbook 1967, page 392. Vigies Ray Bull, Bruce Anderson, Tay Wise, Al Brinkman, Mike Grader, and John Ranck prepare to fire the cannon during Homecoming. The cannon was brought out of retirement for the occasion.

because I was seeing them on behalf of TCU. That was an experience shared among the four of us and also by Bill Slater of the school of communication, who joined us a year later. We all saw our wardrobes shift quickly to purple, and even many of those who we were meeting often donned purple ties or scarves to reciprocate. Though I returned to faculty status in the fall of 2007, purple suits still dominate my wardrobe, and in many circles I remain known as "that woman from TCU."

I witnessed Fort Worth's generosity to TCU over and over again. Small contributions were offered to fund cash prizes for the Creative Writing Awards and larger ones to fund scholarships.

Small donors banded together to endow projects that none could accomplish individually. And, there were the buildings. In the brief decade that I have been at TCU, a new recreation center has replaced the old one, and the new Brown-Lupton University Union has risen on Stadium Drive to anchor the university on the west and create a new commons flanked by four new residence halls. Smith Entrepreneurs Hall and Tucker Technology Center grace the east side of campus. Finally, Scharbauer Hall opened overlooking the commons to house most of AddRan College. Each new edifice represented a financial commitment to the university and an investment in its future,

Yearbook 1950, page 179.
Grouping around the jail.

many made by Fort Worth residents, sometimes with no direct ties to TCU. Various lecture or symposia series were endowed, also by contributions of Fort Worthians. The John V. Roach Honors College replaced the earlier Honors Program, and new initiatives were funded by people, primarily from Fort Worth, who think that TCU remains integral to the future of the city.

Some local foundations have repeatedly answered the call of TCU to improve its facilities and programs. All across campus are reminders of the investments of the Sid Richardson, Burnett, Amon G. Carter, Justin, Lowe, Brown-Lupton, and Rickel foundations, as well as those of alumni and trustees. The synergy between the city and the uni-

versity is palpable on campus and is reflected in the growth of both town and gown.

As the Barnett Shale became viable for natural gas drilling, TCU responded to the absence of geologists and landmen to enable the shale's exploration. The Energy Institute was created and new degree programs instituted to train graduates to work in the energy industry. While the Energy Institute is a recent addition, TCU has produced some of the finest teachers through its College of Education to populate classrooms in Fort Worth and surrounding communities. Likewise, the Neeley School of Business with its emphasis on entrepreneurship, Master of Business Administration, and Master of Accounting degrees has

Yearbook 1995, page 259.
Delta Sigma Theta members
splash around at the car
wash fall fund raiser.

produced well-trained talent necessary for Fort Worth to retain its disproportionate share of Fortune 500 companies. Each of these industries also provided leadership, advice, and money to further the programs.

TCU provides intellectual stimulation to Fort Worth citizens through its Extended Education and Master of Liberal Arts programs, both designed for lifelong learning. Less formal opportunities for intellectual pursuits are available through the rich variety of speakers who are regularly brought to campus. The Schieffer School of Journalism hosts a field of respected journalists each year, and the Speaker Jim Wright Symposium features well-known figures from the political

world. The Ida and Cecil Green Honors Chair program brings noted scholars and visiting authors to campus every week, providing an opportunity for the city to join with students at thought provoking presentations. The TCU Press, with its focus on Texas and Southwestern literature and history, seeks to present the city with the best books to preserve and celebrate the Fort Worth way of life. The presence of foreign students on campus, whether pursuing degrees or studying English in an intensive program, adds a global touch to the city's atmosphere.

TCU has also contributed to the city's commercial life by training individuals in a variety of professional pursuits ranging from interior

Yearbook 1943. 'Good ole' food (P.S. real meal too).

design, public relations, communications, and accounting to computer science, engineering, nurse anesthesia, and speech pathology and audiology. A range of full or part-time graduate programs permits city professionals to hone their skills or develop new ones. Summer institutes, such as the Advanced Placement Summer Institute, bring people from all over the state and sometimes the country to the fair city of Fort Worth.

While TCU continued to blossom, the city of Fort Worth did also, and the two reinforced each other. The Modern Art Museum of Fort Worth, the Kimbell Art Museum, the Amon Carter Museum, the Fort Worth Museum of Science and History, and the National Cowgirl Museum and

Hall of Fame not only draw visitors to the Cultural District but also enrich the lives of residents and offer educational experiences to TCU students. TCU classes in art, literature, history, philosophy, and religion take advantage of the permanent collections and special exhibitions at local museums to illustrate ideas or to provoke critical thinking. Each museum was designed by a notable architect, resulting in an amazing variety of architectural gems. How many universities the size of TCU have access to such a rich cultural heritage only ten minutes from campus?

Fort Worth offers even more for both entertainment and education. In addition to the five museums, the city is also home to a symphony, opera, and ballet. Cowboys and culture mix comfortably, as the Stock Show and Rodeo demonstrate each year. Sundance Square and the Stockyards not only offer entertainment venues but also provide lessons in history and culture. The Sid Richardson Museum, located off Sundance Square, houses an elite collection of art of the American West. Where else but in the Fort Worth Stockyards can one watch a herd of longhorns amble down Exchange Avenue and then step into the Bull Ring for refreshment to find oneself surrounded by Texas art? Restaurants of all varieties not only surround Sundance Square, but also dot the entire city—barbeque, Tex-Mex, nouvelle cuisine, country, haute French cuisine, seafood, Asian, German, urban cowboy, and, of course, Texas steaks and bison burgers.

The city of Fort Worth has attracted other enterprises that also enrich the TCU experience and provide opportunities for research and study. The National Archives and Records Administration Southwest Region and a branch of the United States Mint are located here, both rich resources for students and faculty alike. Likewise, businesses, firms, courts, and other government agencies—local, county, state, and federal—also provide learning experiences for students and research possibilities for faculty. Fort Worth's medical community and major hospitals also have a reciprocal relationship with the university, as students from the Harris College of Nursing and Health Sciences obtain valuable experience during their studies and provide the city a wealth of talented new professionals upon graduation.

Each year TCU brings in approximately 8,500 students, mostly undergraduates, who become Fort Worth consumers, adding not only to the local economy but also to sales tax revenue for the city and other agencies. The university itself had an annual budget of $291 million for the 2009 fiscal year, all of which also fuels Fort Worth's economic engine. It employs 1,850 people, 523 of whom are full-time faculty members, and has an annual payroll of $123 million.

Indeed, a century of partnership has benefited both Texas Christian University and Fort Worth. The two have grown, matured, and flourished together. One can hardly imagine TCU without Fort Worth or Fort Worth without TCU. Each would be poorer without the other. The formula for making this such a positive collaboration has been an attitude that our success is your success. Thank you, Fort Worth. Thank you, TCU.

MARY L. VOLCANSEK
Professor, Political Science
Executive Director, The Center for
Texas Studies at TCU

2

CLOSING THE CIRCLE:
TCU FROM FORT WORTH TO FORT WORTH

GENE ALLEN SMITH

Fire gutted the TCU Main Building on March 23, 1910. By morning all that stood was the shell of the building.

Perhaps the most important event in TCU history occurred on Wednesday, March 23, 1910. During the early evening, just shortly after study hours began, a group of students in the TCU Main Building in Waco smelled smoke. While looking for the source of the smell, someone from the fourth floor suddenly screamed, "Fire, fire! The building is on fire. The whole roof is ablaze." Students began scrambling to save themselves and their possessions. While those students and faculty who lived on the lower floors had the time to remove their belongings, unfortunately those who lived on the fourth floor lost everything to the flames.

When the sun rose the following morning, all that stood was a charred hulk of the former structure. The blaze had completely gutted the brick and wooden building. Classes resumed in a few days in other locations, including in faculty members' homes. Student morale quickly improved as most found alternative living accommodations. The tragedy united TCU students and faculty in a common cause, and even the citizens of Waco and the students at Baylor provided assistance in this hour of need. What no one understood at the time was that this misfortune would foretell great things for the struggling institution founded under the auspices of the Christian Church (Disciples of Christ). On May 10, 1910, less than two months after the disastrous fire, the TCU Board of Trustees signed a contract to return to Fort Worth, ending a thirty-seven-year journey that brought the school back to its roots.

TCU has humble nineteenth-century Fort Worth origins. The TCU-Fort Worth association began when Confederate veteran Addison Clark

ABOVE
Addison (upper) and Randolph (lower) Clark founded the coeducational forerunner to TCU during 1869 in Fort Worth's notorious Hell's Half Acre.

traveled to the city in February 1869 to teach at a small private school started by civic leader John Peter Smith. Clark's younger brother Randolph taught in a nearby Birdville school. But by September 1869, both were in the city and teaching in the reorganized and renamed Male and Female Seminary of Fort Worth. Located on the east side of town near the present-day Santa Fe building, the enterprise sat squarely in the middle of the city's notorious Hell's Half Acre. And despite the "human wreckage and debris," the iniquities that made "days and nights hideous" there in the Acre, the school flourished until the national economic crisis of 1873. Randolph acknowledged the Clarks probably could have survived the economic calamity, but fighting the "whirlpool of licentiousness and greed" that tempted young men

who were "were dazzled by the glitter of vice and caught up like insects around a street light" took too much energy. Concerned for the moral welfare of their young students, the Clark brothers accepted Pleasant Thorp's invitation to move the school to a rural setting some forty miles southwest of Fort Worth.

The Clark brothers' school opened in Thorp Spring on September 1, 1873, and by the following spring they had secured a state charter as AddRan Male and Female College. Hence TCU recognizes 1873 as its official founding date. This coeducational institution was progressive for the era, and its course of study included distinct curricula for men and women and study of the Bible, as well as literary and scientific education. The Thorp Spring location fulfilled the Clark brothers'

FACING PAGE
Pleasant Thorp Building, 1873-1876, that served as the original Thorp Spring building for AddRan Male and Female College.

RIGHT
Ingram Flats, situated at the corner of Fort Worth's Weatherford and Commerce Streets, served as the TCU campus during the 1910-1911 academic year.

wishes to remove students from potential secular temptations; the pastoral location also provided an ideal setting to feed the moral and spiritual hunger of these voracious students. Although Thorp Spring's location provided for the educational and spiritual needs of wayward students, the school's isolation created great financial difficulty. Fort Worth reappeared in the college's history in June 1889 when the Texas Christian Missionary Convention, a state organization of Christian churches, met in the city. At that meeting the Clark brothers gifted their institution to the Christian Church, which officially changed the school's name to AddRan Christian University. The union between the school and the church temporarily solved AddRan Christian University's financial woes, until a new crisis forced the institution to move to another location.

AddRan Christian University moved to Waco in January 1896 because the city of Waco and the Convention of Christian Churches made promises of financial support. Located some three-and-a-half miles north of the railway station, the fifteen-acre Waco campus initially consisted of a large four-story brick and wooden building. Accessible to downtown via streetcar, the school was renamed Texas Christian University in 1902, and grew to include the Main Building, the Girls' Home (dorm), Townsend Memorial Hall (another women's dorm), a gymnasium and natatorium funded by the campus chapter of the YMCA, and a small building that housed the school's heating and lighting plants. Graduating classes had also contributed an entrance arch, a floral court with

This picture, taken circa 1923-24, shows the historic core of the TCU campus. The streetcar running down University Drive did not arrive until 1923, and by 1924 Mary Couts Burnett Library had been constructed on the east side of the street.

for long-time supporters Major J. Jarvis and Mrs. Ida Van Zandt Jarvis, served for the most part as a women's dorm from its opening in 1911 until the building's renovation in 2008; there were brief periods, however, when it served as a dorm for men. For example, from 1942 to 1944 Jarvis Hall housed men involved in the U.S. Navy's V-12 officer training program. Goode Hall, named for Mrs. M. A. Goode of Bartlett, Texas, housed all men until Clark Hall opened in 1913; between 1913 and 1925 Goode Hall housed ministerial and married students.

Goode Hall was demolished in January 1958 for the construction of the present-day Clark Hall. The original Clark Hall was razed in 1959 for construction of present-day Sadler Hall, which opened in 1960. The fifth and sixth buildings constructed as part of the original campus on the west side of modern-day University Drive included Brite College of the Bible (presently the Bailey Building), which opened in 1914, and the gymnasium, which contained a swimming pool (presently the Ballet and Modern Dance Building), completed in 1921.

Yearbook 1922, page 158. The TCU pool was located in the basement of the Gymnasium Building, completed in 1921. This image shows the 1922 women's swimming squad.

FAR RIGHT
TCU agreed to return to Fort Worth because city leaders promised, among other things, to build a streetcar line to campus. Completed in 1923, students could make the one-way trip from campus to downtown in about an hour. The streetcar company also encouraged TCU students to reserve streetcars and interurban trains for special occasions, even decorating them with streamers, banners, and purple Horned Frogs. In the background sits Memorial Arch and the original columned Administration Building, later renovated and renamed Reed Hall.

In an attempt to solidify its educational reputation and broaden its offerings, TCU joined with Fort Worth University in 1911 to provide medical training and education. Although Fort Worth University Medical School had been in operation since 1894, by 1913 TCU had absorbed the medical college and assumed control of its downtown properties. TCU's College of Medicine occupied a facility downtown and also provided students with clinical opportunities at St. Joseph's Infirmary on South Main Street; faculty frequently held clinics at all of the local hospitals. During the early twentieth century, the American Medical Association began demanding higher medical education training standards and financial stability for all schools accredited by the association. And while TCU could boast 350 medical graduates by 1918, the school could not meet AMA standards, forcing trustees to close its facilities. TCU's medical students moved to the Baylor Medical College in Dallas. From 1915 to 1920 TCU also had a School of Law affiliated with AddRan College. Students could earn a BA degree in law through AddRan in three years or the LLB from AddRan and the School of Law in six years. Again, because the university could not meet the increased professionalization and financial standards imposed by the American Bar Association, TCU closed the law school in 1920. Both experiments at professional education fell victim to the growing professional standards instituted by national organizations as well as to the financial instability faced by the university during its early years in Fort Worth.

When the campus opened in 1911, a single gravel street called Forest Park Boulevard connected TCU with downtown. The road ran along present-day Forest Park, Park Hill Drive, and then south along present-day University Drive to the south end of the TCU campus. A simple gravel drive ran in front of TCU buildings, providing parking space for the few cars on cam-

FACING PAGE (UPPER)
TCU's 1915 track team posing for a picture on the west side of Goode Hall (on right) and Administration Building (on left).

FACING PAGE (LOWER)
The 1916 TCU football squad, coached by former fullback Milton Daniel, was among the best teams of the early era. The team finished with a season record of 6-2-1.

RIGHT
TCU vs. Carruthers Field (U.S. pilots training at nearby Benbrook), October 5, 1918, played on the site of the current TCU Library. The pilots won the game 7-6.

pus. Otherwise, little, if anything, marred the vistas from TCU; to the east one could easily see the Frisco railroad line more than a mile away, while to the south and west lay nothing but unbroken and open prairies as far as the eye could see. The first paved street to TCU arrived in 1923, a decade after the university's return, and with it came a residential building boom between Cantey Street and Park Hill Drive. Shortly thereafter, a streetcar line ran in the middle of the road to campus, as agreed upon in Fort Worth's original proposal to lure TCU to Fort Worth.

In 1916, the university acquired land to the east of University Drive as far as Lubbock Street and between Lowden and Bowie Streets and began using this site for athletic fields. The university played football there from 1916 until the construction of the TCU library in 1924. The university immediately christened Clark Field to the south and east of the library, where football was played until October 11, 1930, when TCU opened Amon G. Carter Stadium with a 40-0

defeat of the University of Arkansas. The university also joined the nascent Southwest Conference in 1923, and, during the following decade, its football program blossomed. In fact, TCU was one of only three schools across the country—the others were Notre Dame and the University of Texas—to have a perfect regular season record of 9-0. By 1929, TCU had won its first Southwest Conference championship and finished seventh in the Associated Press (AP) poll. The team's success brought thousands of spectators to the games, including a reported crowd of 20,000 for a 1927 campus contest against Texas A&M.

TCU had found a permanent home in Fort Worth, and the city had found a winning football team. The union between the two solidified. During the 1930s, the city became Frog crazy, and there was no bigger fan than businessman Amon G. Carter, publisher and founder of the *Fort Worth Star-Telegram*, who saw TCU's and Fort Worth's fates as interconnected. He promoted both tirelessly, which was easy while the football

FACING PAGE (UPPER)
TCU played its football games on site of the TCU Library (under construction) on the east side of University Drive, from 1916 until 1924, when it joined the Southwest Conference and moved to nearby Clark Field.

FACING PAGE (LOWER)
Young women playing basketball on courts in front of the Gymnasium Building, circa 1923. Note the crowd of spectators in the shadows as the streetcar passes.

RIGHT
Football put TCU and Fort Worth on the map. By the mid-1930s the city had become Frog crazy and there was no bigger fan than Star-Telegram founder and businessman Amon G. Carter.

FAR RIGHT
In 1938, TCU quarterback Davey O'Brien was named to thirteen All-America teams, and he became the first college football player to win the Heisman, Maxwell, and Walter Camp awards in the same year. When he went to New York to accept the Heisman Trophy, Fort Worth boosters hired a stagecoach to transport him to the Downtown Athletic Club.

team continued winning. TCU won Southwest Conference Football Championships again in 1932 and 1938 and claimed national championships in 1935 and 1938, the year that TCU quarterback Davey O'Brien won the fourth Heisman Trophy.

Despite athletic success, TCU's early years remained marred by financial insecurity that did not disappear until December 1923, when the university received a contribution of nearly $3,000,000 from Mary Couts Burnett. Although she had no connection to TCU, rumors abounded that she gave the donation to spite her deceased husband, cattleman Samuel Burk Burnett, who had refused on several occasions to support the university. Burk claimed that Mary had been suffering hallucinations and had threatened to harm herself. He had her declared legally insane, confined to a private home in Weatherford, and then changed his will to disinherit her. When he died suddenly in 1922, Mary escaped her confinement, returned to Fort Worth, had her

insanity ruling overturned, and challenged her late husband's will. Awarded half of her husband's six million dollar fortune, she decided to bequeath her estate to TCU, with the provision that $150,000 of the total be allocated for a library—the first building constructed on the east side of present-day University Drive. This contribution, at the time one of the largest ever given to an educational institution in Texas, ensured the survival of the little school on the hill.

Except for the construction of Mary Couts Burnett Library and Amon G. Carter Stadium, TCU saw little growth or expansion during the 1920s and 1930s. When President McGruder Ellis Sadler arrived at TCU in April 1941, he acknowledged that the university needed to bolster its infrastructure. He embarked on an aggressive building program that spanned his two decades of service. A women's dorm, Foster Hall, opened in June 1942 as the first building on campus with a gabled red clay tile roof; this pattern then became standard for campus construction and renovations

Mary Couts Burnett had no association to TCU when she contributed some $3,000,000 to the university in December 1923. Her donation assured the financial survival of the university.

RIGHT
Mary Couts Burnett Library, constructed in 1924 from the largest donation that the university had ever received. One stipulation of the Burnett donation required that $150,000 be allotted to the construction of a library building.

across TCU. Waits Hall for women and Tom Brown dorm for men (now the site of the Tom Brown/Pete Wright Residential Community constructed in 1999) both opened during the fall of 1947, and represented the first new buildings constructed after World War II. The university increased the size of Amon G. Carter Stadium to 25,000 seats in 1947, to 33,500 in 1948, and in 1956 built an upper deck and press box that increased seating to more than 47,000. In December 1949, a fine arts building, Ed Landreth Hall, opened as the first building on campus with air conditioning and the first permanent building

constructed on campus for instructional purposes since 1921.

Sadler's second phase of construction during the 1950s included the air-conditioned Winton-Scott Hall of Science (summer of 1952), the New England-inspired pink brick Robert Carr Chapel (spring 1954) that departed from the university's buff brick style, and the original Brown-Lupton Student Center (January 1955). Dan Rogers Hall (summer 1957) accommodated an emerging school of business, the Mary Couts Burnett expansion (winter 1958) tripled the size of the library, and the construction of Sadler Hall

From 1924 until October 1930, TCU football played its home games on Clark Field, to the south and east of the current Mary Couts Burnett Library. During that period the football program blossomed (47 wins, five losses, and five ties). TCU was one of only three schools—the others were Notre Dame and the University of Texas—to have a perfect regular season record of 9-0. In 1929, during its last season on Clark Field, TCU won its first Southwest Conference championship and finished seventh in the AP poll. Amon G. Carter Stadium opened on October 11, 1930, with TCU thrashing the University of Arkansas 40-7.

(September 1960) provided for a new administration building. The renovation of the former Administration Building, renamed Dave C. Reed Hall in May 1961, created space for AddRan College. Daniel-Meyer Coliseum (December 1961) provided seating for 7,000 for sporting events, convocations, conventions, and commencement programs; the outer concourse offered space for student registration well into the 1970s. Perhaps one of TCU's more obscure operations was a small airport, the runway of which ran parallel to the east side of Hulen Street, south of

the current I-20 highway; the entrance to the airport was located at the intersection of Wedgmont Circle North and Granbury Road, some five miles south of campus. Established during the mid-1940s, the airport was used to support flight training for the university's Air Force ROTC students until it closed in 1957.

TCU's student enrollment also blossomed during the 1950s—by 1960 enrollment topped 8,300 students. This growth, combined with deteriorating student housing, convinced President Sadler of the need for renovated and new dorms.

Bandstand in front of Jarvis Hall. Though its appearance has been modified through several renovations since the day this photo was taken, Jarvis is one of the few original buildings remaining on campus.

Three new dorms—Pete Wright (1955), Milton Daniel (1957), and Clark Hall (1959)—provided space for men, while two dorms—Colby D. Hall (1957) and Andrew Sherley (1958)—offered housing for women. The R.M. Means Apartments (1959) at the corner of University Drive and Park Hill provided accommodations for married students. Sadler's acquisition of the 106-acre Worth Hills addition offered room to expand over several decades. In fact, Worth Hills has provided the space for seven Greek dorms, the university physical plant, student intramural fields, tennis complex, soccer and baseball fields, and the track and field complex. When the Sadler era ended in 1965, TCU had become a modern university with thirty-four major buildings and covered some two hundred forty acres.

In October 1960, for the fiftieth anniversary of TCU's return to Fort Worth, the *Fort Worth Star-Telegram* and the *Fort Worth Press* published sections on the institution's history and partnership of the school and the city. One statement signed by nine members of the city council concluded:

From 1910, when the city of Fort Worth first donated land for the Texas Christian University campus to the present, University and City have worked in close harmony in building a greater Fort Worth. Such cooperation will continue as Texas Christian University and the City of Fort Worth gird to meet the challenge of service that the next fifty years will bring.

During the second fifty years, Sadler's successors—James M. Moudy, William E. Tucker, Michael R. Ferrari, and Victor J. Boschini—have built upon the successes of their predecessors. Moudy greatly improved the academic standing of the institution and of the faculty by hiring more professors with terminal degrees and implementing six PhD programs across campus. Chancellor Tucker bolstered the institution's financial stability during his almost two decades of leadership, greatly increasing the value of the endowment. Dr. Ferrari's short tenure provided visionary planning and leadership, laying the foundation for

Flowers and trees line the entrance to Sadler Hall. While TCU's landscaping plan may have changed since this image was captured, flowers and plants remain an important part of the manicured and modern university.

the twenty-first century, while Chancellor Boschini has implemented a building program that would rival Sadler's.

As we celebrate a century of TCU in Fort Worth, the university encompasses 271 acres in a largely residential neighborhood five miles from the heart of downtown Fort Worth. The institution has invested more than $500 million in new facilities and in upgrading residence halls, classrooms, laboratories, and sporting facilities. During the 2009 college football season, Fort Worth once again became Frog crazy. *ESPN College Game-Day* traveled to Fort Worth, and a record-setting crowd and a national television audience watched as the Horned Frogs dismantled the Utah Utes. As the season concluded and the possibility of TCU participating in a Bowl Championship Series bowl game (ultimately the Tostitos Fiesta Bowl) grew even greater, downtown buildings sported purple lights, citizens talked endlessly about TCU's season prospects, and city leaders publicly

supported the team and even colored the Trinity River purple. This fervent atmosphere harkened back to the 1930s and the days of Sammy Baugh and Davey O'Brien.

As TCU and Fort Worth begin their second century of partnership, both are poised for an exciting future. TCU's circuitous journey from Fort Worth to Thorp Spring to Waco and back to Fort Worth created a resilience and determination to survive and prosper. Meanwhile, TCU's connection to Fort Worth helped create a vibrant and attractive educational institution and a progressive city that is considered one of the most livable in America. Continued future cooperation can only mean greater things—for both TCU and Fort Worth!

GENE ALLEN SMITH
Professor of History
Director, The Center for Texas Studies at TCU

3

IMPRESSIONS OF ACADEMICS AT TCU DURING THE LAST 100 YEARS

BOB J. FRYE

Paul Wassenich, renowned for his interest in human values, religion professor, and founder of the TCU Honors Program.

My arrival at Texas Christian University in 1966 seemed inauspicious. Let me explain. As a brand-new faculty member needing advice from my English Chairman (the title then), one day in September—that's when the fall term began then—I parked my 1956 Ford in the faculty parking lot in front of the Brown-Lupton Student Center. I climbed two floors to the English Department Office in Reed 215 and asked to see Dr. Cecil Williams, the man who had interviewed me at the annual Modern Language Association meeting in Chicago in December of 1965 and who was, except for Public Relations Director Amos Melton, the only person at TCU that I had come to know. The secretary quietly answered, "Dr. Williams died last evening." I did not believe my ears and repeated my request only to hear again, "Dr. Williams died last evening. He collapsed after

mowing his lawn." Totally abashed and only slightly calmed by Jim Corder, who said he had just been named Acting Chairman but didn't know what to do yet, I returned to my car only to find a TCU parking ticket on my windshield.

Consequently one of my first duties as a new faculty member of English in 1966 was to attend the funeral of the man who had hired me. Within two weeks that fall, I attended funerals for both TCU Chancellor Emeritus M. E. Sadler and, six days later, Amos Melton, Public Relations Director. Initially I had to wonder if TCU were the right place for me. But it has been, and more.

I missed the first ninety-three years of TCU's existence, but with the help of histories by Jerome Moore, Colby Hall, Libby Proffer, and Joan Swaim, interviews with colleagues, and other sources, I have been able to learn much about the

Yearbook 1922, page 104.
The Board of Trustees of TCU.

rich academic life of TCU before I arrived and got my parking ticket. Moreover, I have personally experienced more than forty-three additional years of that history. Although my focus is on the 100 years since TCU moved from Waco to Fort Worth following the well-documented fire in 1910, I have learned that Fort Worth has been, in fact, central to the university's evolution from the very beginning. Addison and Randolph Clark began a school in Fort Worth even before the establishment of AddRan Male and Female College at Thorp Spring in 1873. Moreover, the university's connection with the Christian Church (Disciples of Christ) has been significant from the beginning. Addison Clark and Colonel John Peter Smith ran a private school connected, Jerome Moore writes in *A Hundred Years of History,* "both physically and spiritually to the First Christian Church" of

Fort Worth. When Smith left the school in 1869, Randolph Clark joined his brother, Addison, to found the Male and Female Seminary of Fort Worth. As Colby Hall observes in *History of Texas Christian University,* "In a very genuine sense Texas Christian University was born in Fort Worth in the year 1869," even though Moore notes that the Clark brothers labeled 1873-74, in their first catalog at Thorp Spring after leaving Fort Worth, as the initial session of their college.

The return of TCU to Fort Worth in 1910 essentially completed the circle.

Arriving in 1966, I was assigned Office 221 in Reed Hall, which, I have learned from Joan Swaim and others, was the original Administration Building on the new Fort Worth campus when TCU moved from Waco in 1910. Providing impressions of TCU academics from this historical place has its advantages, and my service as Chair of the TCU Faculty Senate (1981-82), coach of the first TCU women's varsity basketball team (1974-75), active contributor to the TCU Honors Program, participant in every single TCU commencement ceremony but six since I arrived, and TCU English professor now in my forty-fourth year—well, I have had extraordinary opportunities to view all sides of TCU, especially its academics.

Two facts dominate my impressions of the history of TCU's years before I arrived: the early focus on liberal arts education and the connection with the Disciples of Christ Church. The charter of the Clark brothers' college in Thorp Spring adopted in 1874 stresses liberal arts: "The purpose of said College shall be for the support and promotion of Literary and Scientific Education..." That the university maintained this emphasis on liberal arts in all those years before I arrived in 1966 is clearly evident from the selection of TCU, in 1971, for a chapter of Phi Beta Kappa. As the PBK homepage reveals, the society "celebrates and advocates excellence in the liberal arts and sciences" and embraces "the principles of freedom of inquiry and liberty of thought and expression." This selection affirmed the high academic standards at TCU, well illustrated by Dean Colby Hall's being chosen, for thirteen years straight, as Chair of the Committee on Standards of the accrediting agency, Association of Texas Colleges, of which TCU became a charter member in 1912.

Some have expressed concern about the "C" in TCU through the years. Indeed, one recent PhD department's ad for a faculty position describes TCU as "a private, secular institution," which hardly honors our institution's long association with but definitely not government by the Disciples of Christ Church. In light of this concern, it may be useful to note this statement from the

Clark brothers' 1875 catalogue: "The institution is not conducted on any narrow, sectional, or sectarian principle; but relying upon Him who rules and guides all things well, nothing shall be left undone that we can do to make the enterprise meet the expectations of those desiring a thorough education." Chancellor Emeritus William Tucker clearly illuminates this long and important relationship between TCU and the Disciples of Christ Church in "Muddle in the Middle: The 'C' in TCU," a *TCU Magazine* article from 2001. When I discussed this issue with Dean Emeritus Michael McCracken, who came to TCU in 1971 and served as dean for twenty-seven years first of the AddRan College of Arts and Sciences and then of the College of Engineering and Sciences, he shared this succinct response from Dr. Tucker as to what the "C" in TCU means: "Christianity will get a fair hearing in the marketplace of ideas."

Having an office in Reed Hall for forty years has given me an uncommonly helpful perspective on TCU academics during the 100 years that TCU has been in Fort Worth. As Joan Swaim points out in *Walking TCU,* "nearly every academic program on the campus began instruction in this building." Under Edward Waits' presidency (1916-41) and more especially during Dr. M. E. Sadler's presidency (1941-65), the TCU curriculum I found here in 1966 had been shaped into six units: AddRan College of Arts and Sciences, School of Fine Arts, School of Education, Graduate School, The Evening College, and Brite College of the Bible. The year I came, a faculty leave-with-pay policy was adopted, and I, for example, have been granted five paid leaves, including a paid "terminal leave"—not a felicitous phrase—when I retired in 2003 before TCU hired me back. It is a policy that has well supported the teacher/scholar model at TCU. The 1960s and early 1970s were, of

Wassenich was a frequent founder—after two degrees from the University of Chicago, in 1946, he was the founding pastor of University Christian Church in Austin; in 1963, the founder of the TCU Honors Program; in 1967, he was the principal founder of the TCU Faculty Senate. Following his retirement in 1976 from the Religion Department of TCU, he founded an orchard out at Weatherford which produced luscious peaches, of which some of us ate so many that, like a horse, we foundered on them—the *OED* also defines founder as "to burst" or "fall helplessly down." A cardboard side from a box of Wassenich peaches sits in my study on a bookshelf to remind me of those marvelous peaches and, more particularly, of that marvelous man, Paul Wassenich. The cardboard piece reads: "ONE PECK / WASSENICH ORCHARD / STAR RT BOX 743 / MINERAL WELLS, TX. / 325-3076."

The TCU Honors Program Wassenich Founders Medal, established in 1997 to honor Dr. Wassenich, is presented annually to an honors student who has cogently demonstrated, through substantial scholarly achievement, the intellectual values of Dr. Wassenich. Those values always stressed interdisciplinary study and learning and making that learning the vehicle for the formation of values that would reflect the character of Dr. Wassenich who, in his TCU retirement citation of 1976, was described as "the moral center of TCU." It has been my special privilege to present the Wassenich Award at each Honors Banquet since 2005.

course, a tumultuous time in American history with civil rights marches and Vietnam War protests dominating the news. I found it to be an exciting time to be at TCU, for I discovered the Fort Worth campus to be an intellectually alive place. Students and faculty seemed energetically engaged, although I saw a sign my first week on the second floor of Reed Hall that read: "Apathy Rally Canceled Due to Lack of Interest." But I soon learned of the new Honors Program and the new Faculty Senate and the new Faculty Assembly. And then I, a twenty-six-year-old newly minted PhD, met a man who became one of my heroes, Dr. Paul Wassenich.

The Oxford English Dictionary defines founder as one who "sets up or establishes for the first time; one who builds on a firm ground or base; who constructs on a principle." Paul

I soon learned of three other legendary TCU professors—Mabel Major, Lorraine Sherley, and Willis Hewatt. All three were named Minnie Stevens Piper Professors, one of the top ten professors of Texas—Major in 1964, Sherley in 1965, and Hewatt in 1969. Miss Sherley—the way many

FACING PAGE (UPPER)
Yearbook 1986, page 5.
Professors congregate outside
Ed Landreth Hall.

FACING PAGE (LOWER)
Lorraine Sherley, beloved
Shakespeare teacher,
renowned for her course
on the interrelationship
of the arts.

RIGHT
Yearbook 1967, page 30.
Forty-five contestants pose
on steps of Ed Landreth,
where flags of their countries
flew during the event.

addressed her although in 1971 TCU conferred on her the honorary Doctor of Letters—taught her famous Interrelation of the Arts, Shakespeare, and other English courses for forty-four years (1927-71). "Feared and revered," she was in charge of sophomore English in 1966 when I arrived. When our ordered textbooks were late, Miss Sherley, dressed in pink tennis shoes but commanding re spect and attention wherever she appeared (her 1955 Chevy was never ticketed), told me simply to "ditto" (copy) materials for the students to read. I did so, baptizing my hands and face with purple ink—a badge, then, of active teaching. Two years ago, Paige Miller, Miss Sherley's great-great-niece from Anna, Texas, was one of the best students in my Major British Writers class. I told Paige that Miss Sherley once asked me, in 1970, to write the TCU Theatre notes for Shakespeare's *Twelfth Night*. At thirty years old, I did Miss Sherley's assignment with fear and trembling, but when I asked her what she thought of my printed notes

for the TCU production during Festival Arts Week, she succinctly replied, "They are excellent." Mark Twain says that you can live a month on a compliment; I have been living over forty-three years on Miss Sherley's compliment. Even as I write these words, I am holding in my lap a copy of Emile Legouis and Louis Cazamian's *A History of English Literature* (1935). On the inside cover, in the upper left corner, is a left-hand-written, in red, tiny but distinct "L. Sherley." Miss Sherley died on February 29, 1984. The TCU Faculty Senate passed a resolution the next day composed by Betsy Colquitt and presented by me on Betsy's behalf. It included this statement: "As student, alumna, and faculty member, Miss Sherley epitomized the best in herself, and in her the University discovered an emblem of its own excellence."

After J. Frank Dobie's course at the University of Texas, TCU in Fort Worth was the second university in Texas to offer an English course in Southwest American literature. Mabel Major,

Betsy Colquitt, professor of English, teaching with her uncommon grace the modern poetry class.

teaching, as Lorraine did, forty-four years (1919-63), took that course to new heights, publishing with Rebecca Lee Smith of TCU and T. M. Pierce of the University of New Mexico *Southwest Heritage: A Literary History with Bibliography* (3rd ed., 1972). In an essay in *Celebrating 100 Years of the Texas Folklore Society, 1909-2009,* Joyce Roach credits Miss Major—"I never did call her Professor"—for inspiring her with keen, thoughtful advice and quotes J. Frank Dobie's high praise

of her. In 1964, the same year she was named a Piper Professor of Texas, TCU awarded her an honorary Doctor of Letters. Her niece, Mary Bush, speaks of the students' extraordinary admiration for Miss Major, and Chancellor Sadler observed on her retirement that "it is easier for me to think of the University without my connection with it than to think of it without Miss Major actively connected to its program."

F. L. Abernethy of the Texas Folklore Society—Miss Major was president of it in 1936—described her as "a feisty and formidable maiden lady on one level, but smiling warmth on another." Emeritus Professor of Geology Art Ehlmann, an invaluable colleague and candid friend, recently told me this anecdote about Miss Major. He said he had received a phone call many years ago from Sylvia Gilmartin of the TCU library, asking him to put in a request for Larry McMurtry's novel *Horseman, Pass By.* When Art asked why, Sylvia explained that an English professor had kept that book checked out because she did not think the language appropriate for TCU students. Art identified that professor as Mabel Major. He promptly honored Sylvia's request. I will add only that in the early 1960s both McMurtry and the renowned John Graves taught English at TCU. In 1983, TCU conferred the honorary Doctor of Letters on Graves; I had the honor of composing the citation.

A third legendary professor at TCU I learned about early in my career here was Willis Hewatt. After Dr. W. M. Winton of the Department of Geology and Biology had chaired the TCU Pre-Medical Committee from 1913-50, Dr. Hewatt succeeded him and chaired it from 1950-73. He was extremely selective in admitting students to the pre-med program, so much so that he apparently had a 100 percent acceptance rate of TCU

FAR RIGHT
Yearbook 1986, page 114.
Editorial Assistant Scott
Ewoldsen.

RIGHT
Willis G. Hewatt, chair of
biology department, uncom-
monly influential pre-med
advisor, and competitive
handball player.

students into medical school. A high acceptance rate continued when he was succeeded as pre-med advisor by Professor Manny Reinecke, who did significant research into the medicinal properties of plants, and then by Professor Phillip Hartman, whose research on worms (*C. elegans*) is widely known at TCU.

Reportedly Dr. Hewatt regularly defeated his son-in-law, former All-Southwest Conference guard at TCU and varsity basketball coach, Johnny Swaim, on the handball court. In addition to receiving the Piper Award, Dr. Hewatt, along with Lorraine Sherley, was named one of three Foundation Members of the new chapter of Phi Beta Kappa on campus in 1971.

I was pleased to come to TCU just as the new Honors Program was in its beginning. Mark Wassenich, son of Dr. Paul Wassenich, has told me that while he rode with his dad, carpooling with Dr. James Moudy, he overheard them often discussing the prospects for an honors program. With Dr. Moudy's strong administrative encouragement, Dr. Wassenich founded the program in

1962. There had earlier been "Invitation Sections" of classes and Alpha Chi Professors of the Year awards dating from 1957: Lorraine Sherley (1958), Marguerite Potter of history, later coach of TCU's GE College Bowl Team (1959), Paul Wassenich (1963)—a year after founding the new program with Dr. Moudy's help—and Betsy Colquitt of English (1965), just before I arrived. Betsy wrote a play instead of giving the traditional honors lecture, deflecting the focus from herself to the student performers, quite typical of her genuine, gracious modesty. I learned soon that Honors Convocations in the spring semester at eleven o'clock on Thursday mornings were well attended, followed by a two o'clock "Forum" in the afternoon with the invited speaker, and then an evening honors banquet where the previous year's recipient of the "Faculty Recognition Award" would give an address.

Extraordinary, gifted speakers inspired us at Honors Convocations. Here is a sampling: Dr. Paul Lang, Avalon Professor in Humanities, Columbia, on "Words and Music" (1970);

Yearbook 1971, page 41.
College Bowl State Champs.

Pulitzer Prize winner N. Scott Momaday, "Indian Oral Tradition" (1973); Loren Eiseley, Benjamin Franklin Professor, Anthropology and the History of Science, University of Pennsylvania, "Man Against the Universe" (1976); Pulitzer Prize winner Edward Albee, "The Playwright vs. The Theatre" (1983); Stephen Jay Gould, Harvard, "The Individual in Darwin's World" (1987); and artfully introduced by Professor Betsy Colquitt, the thirty-ninth U.S. Poet Laureate Robert Pinsky, Boston University, "Learning and Art" (2000). In 1977, composer and Pulitzer Prize winner Howard Hanson, following the TCU Concert Chorale's singing of Hanson's "How Excellent Thy Name" under the direction of the late Ron Shirey, remarked that this rendition of his work was the best he had ever heard.

Honors Day, for me, remains the high feast day of the academic year. Under the direction first of Paul Wassenich, then Ted Klein, Fred Erisman, Keith Odom, Jim Kelly, David Grant, Kathryn McDorman, and the current dean of the new John

V. Roach Honors College, Peggy Watson, the opportunities for intellectual engagement and learning have been superb. The Honors Day Banquet, with the Honors Professor of the Year's talk, the recognition of the Senior Honors Scholars from every department, the Sigma Xi and Phi Beta Kappa special senior awards—well, it is, for me, not to be missed. The Honors Day program lists all the honor societies for various disciplines. Mortar Board was originally all female—the 1971 program says "Senior Women"—until 1975 following enactment of Title IX. It recognizes students demonstrating distinction in leadership, scholarship, and service. I served as the first male sponsor of Mortar Board in 1981 and member Paul Gorman was the first male president.

Under the leadership, especially, of Dr. Jim Kelly, the Honors Program developed sequences of courses to complement the four core colloquia. These courses were team-taught. When Professor Tom Copeland, a dear colleague of mine in English, died unexpectedly in August of 1987, Dr. Kelly asked me to succeed Tom in the Honors Humanities Sequence as the literature person. I found the prospect terrifying, for I knew the high scholarly levels of which Tom and his colleagues in the sequence were capable, but I worked hard with the team of Michael Winesanker (Music), David Grant (Religion), Mark Thistlethwaite (Art History), and John Bohon (History). For nine years it was the most intellectually exciting time of my life at TCU (1987-96).

Complementing the Honors Program were the Brachman Living-Learning Residence Hall (1970) and the Tom Brown/Jarvis experiment in the seventies and eighties. In the latter, these two dormitories developed a library, a *Portable Tom Brown,* a program of Dorm Dons (I was one), and in general offered a sense of independent intellectual engagement. But that is not to say that the

Betsy Colquitt, considered by many one of the best poets in Texas.

sixties and seventies were without their controversies. I remember reading in the *TCU Daily Skiff* in 1974 about unabashed streakers flashing past Associate Dean of Students Buck Beneze. While his retirement citation notes that Buck had compassionately given, up to that point, sixteen gallons as a generous blood donor, he was not happy with those students zipping by him, as he ironically said, "buck-naked." Moreover, when Jack Cogdill, Chair of the Theatre Department and Honors Professor of the Year in 1969, gave his Honors Banquet address, "Fish-Keeping," in 1970, he severely criticized the TCU administration. Vice Chancellor James Newcomer, in the audience, appeared surprised by the address. I was sitting by Professor Comer Clay, Chair of the TCU Faculty Senate, who observed: "He made the points pretty well, don't you think?"

There was a period in the late sixties and early to mid-seventies during which Chancellor Moudy declared a "financial exigency" and curtailed most raises, especially for faculty and staff. For example, the headline above the fold for the March 13, 1970, *Skiff* declared in large boldface type: "FACULTY DENIED RAISE: Moudy Calls for Restraints in Hiring, Pay Increases Here." Rita Emrigh's front-page article begins: "Chancellor James M. Moudy rocked faculty and staff, complaining of an overpopulation of faculty and expressing disappointment in the learning experiences available here, in a Tuesday speech in the Student Center ballroom, presenting the recommended 1970-71 budget." I vividly remember that speech; I was there. And I remember, too, the hush that fell over the room as the "cut-down expenses" budget was explained and then how a tall,

Yearbook 1986, page 141. Resisting strong wind, members of Mortar Board, the honor society for seniors, walk to Robert Carr Chapel for the annual initiation ceremony.

thin colleague, the courageous, plain-spoken Art Ehlmann of the Geology Department, rose to ask this question: "Dr. Moudy, do you have a proportionate reduction in the administrative salaries?" I do not recall the Chancellor's answer, but the *Skiff's* report concludes with this account: "When one faculty member asked if the administration could have frozen hiring altogether and given the staff a slight general increase, Dr. Moudy said he felt a 1 or 2 percent increase would have gone over as unenthusiastically as the zero percent increase. 'Try us,' the member replied, and the staff applauded."

As Art and I visited about this experience recently, we both agreed that Dr. Moudy, as a pastor, certainly must have felt he was doing the very best he could for his flock. Indeed, Joan Swaim, describing the 1982 Moudy Building of Visual Arts, provides a keen summary of Dr. Moudy's extraordinary leadership and his focus on a

"strengthened academic program," noting that in 1979 the university "further recognized his devoted and able leadership by conferring the honorary Doctor of Laws."

Having missed only six commencements during some forty-three years at TCU, I have always enjoyed watching thousands of students receive their diplomas, including our two daughters, Cynthia (1984) and Brenda (1987), and my wife, Alice (1988), whom I fondly call my TCU roommate. I still have our eight-year-old Cynthia's penciled portrait of President Lyndon Johnson on the back of her May 1968 commencement program when Johnson spoke here and received an honorary Doctor of Laws degree, one of eight honorary degrees bestowed that day. I recall one year when the candidates for graduation kept stumbling over the carpet and a commencement marshal motioned for me to stand on the carpet to hold it down and prevent an accident; it was a long two hours. In

ABOVE
Yearbook 1986, page 143.
Chancellor Tucker presents
the long-awaited sheepskin
as well as a few words of
congratulation to a graduating
senior.

ABOVE RIGHT
Yearbook 1986, page 101.
Members of Mortar Board
cross University Drive on
their way to initiation at
Robert Carr Chapel. They
are led by Jack Larson carry-
ing the Mortar Board banner.

1974, when TCU conferred the honorary Doctor of Letters on Mary Elizabeth Waits Williams, the ubiquitous, remarkable Linda Kaye took my picture, in full academic regalia, with this witty, delightful daughter of "Prexy" Waits who had led TCU from 1916 to 1941, thus helping a young associate professor connect with TCU's historic past.

I recall watching with uncommon admiration Pete Larson, *summa cum laude* in philosophy and mathematics, TCU's only Rhodes scholar, receive his diploma in 1976. Suzanne Drouet from Louisiana, one of six Truman scholars at TCU; thirteen organ students of Emmet Smith, Professor of Music and himself a Fulbright scholar, receiving Fulbrights; Kate Bretscher, a Marshall scholar; Jason Thomas, a Gates scholar; Sandra Doan and Paul Sanchez, both piano performance majors and Fulbright scholars in 2006—all these students I got to see at TCU commencements. M. J. Neeley, founder of the M. J. Neeley School of Business,

Chair of the Board of Trustees, and whose wife, Alice, generously brought the Starpoint School to our campus, used to joke that he did not have a formal education—he was a graduate of Texas A&M! Certainly the graduates I have just named demonstrate clearly that they have received exceptional formal undergraduate educations at TCU.

And when Bruce Capehart (*cum laude*, biology/chemistry) crossed the stage in 1987, I fondly recalled how he and three other students from my honors freshman composition class knocked lightly on my door across from the campus at five one morning; they knew that I regularly rose at four-thirty to grade papers. They had brought hot, steaming chocolate chip cookies, and so I got some milk and shared cookies and milk with them in the circle of light by my grading lamp in our living room. I made clear that this thoughtful act would have no bearing on their grades.

In 1975, I remember Isaac Bashevis Singer,

ABOVE
Yearbook 1969, page 116.
Graduation. Record number of
graduates. Commencement on June 4.
More than 900 earned degrees.

ABOVE RIGHT
A happy day when Mary Beth
Williams received her honorary
doctorate. Bob Frye helps her
celebrate. Courtesy of Bob Frye.

BELOW
Yearbook 1986, page 114.

later Nobel Laureate in literature, receiving an honorary Doctor of Laws degree here and the wonderful party at Professor Betsy Colquitt's home afterward. Seven years later I composed the citation for Norman Cousins' honorary Doctor of Humane Letters; my good friend and generous colleague Jim Corder and I had nominated him in the Faculty Senate. In 1986, Ernest Boyer gave one of the most memorable commencement addresses, "Remembering a Teacher," before receiving his honorary Doctor of Laws. Selected by his peers as the "nation's leading educator," Boyer was interviewed by my daughter Brenda for one of her graphic design assignments. However, while these were all memorable speakers, they do not compare with my experience recorded in my handwritten program notes at the May 1997 TCU commencement when CBS correspondent Bob Schieffer spoke and recalled "when both Exxon and Ross Perot were humble." That day, under the Amon G. Carter Stadium stands as we were lining up in preparation for the graduation ceremony, a

young man walked up to me in his academic robe and said, "You don't know me, but five years ago in El Paso [I was there as the faculty speaker for the Admissions Office "TCU Today" recruiting program.] I talked to you about coming to TCU to be a sports trainer and you went back and talked to Ross Bailey on my behalf. Now I am finishing up as a sports trainer. I've worked for the Houston Oilers and will work here locally for a year and then get my master's and eventually work for a pro sports team. I want to thank you for your important help." I was flabbergasted by these grateful words, and my mind darted to Robert Guerra from San Antonio. He had been our trainer in 1974-75 when I coached the TCU women's basketball team, then earned his master's following his graduation from TCU, and now serves as personal trainer to His Royal Highness, Sultan bin Abdulaziz, Crown Prince of Saudi Arabia.

Despite my seemingly inauspicious beginning at TCU in 1966, I have thoroughly enjoyed my opportunities to teach and write and learn in the

ABOVE
Yearbook 1986, page 143.
A sea of mortarboards listens
while University officials
impart their last words of
wisdom.

ABOVE RIGHT
Yearbook 1986, page 130.

nurturing academic environment here. I have met talented colleagues like Don Jackson of Political Science, yet another Piper Professor who has shown incredible initiative to bring about the Washington Internship Program, the Martin Luther King Jr. Scholarship, the TCU-in-Britain Program, the London Center, and still other initiatives. Don Worcester of the History Department was an incredible teacher/scholar who once showed me, on the Brown-Lupton Student Center steps, his new book on Indians, which had just been published in German. Even after retirement, he went to his TCU office in Reed across from the English Department every day. During the Christmas break when almost everyone was gone, I would go check my mailbox and Don's door to his messy, crowded, but effectively used office would invariably be open. One year it was closed as I walked by in December. But the sign on his door showed he had earlier been there: "Gone home. Too damned cold." His colleague, the holder of the first LBJ Chair, Paul Boller, continues to amaze us all by his publications on American presidents, even at ninety-three. In February 2010,

the first Paul F. Boller Jr. Symposium on the American Presidency featured author/historian Michael Beschloss. Paul is one of my heroes, as is the late Betsy Colquitt who once, at a Saturday morning breakfast at our home, sat on our living room floor in the midst of TCU honors freshman composition students, talking about revising one of her poems over and over.

Another of my exemplars is the late George Tade, Professor of Speech Communications and Dean of the College of Fine Arts, whose eulogy at the memorial service of Professor Mike Winesanker of Music remains one of the finest orations I have ever heard. And I cannot forget that extraordinary gentleman in the white cowboy hat, John Merrill, Director of the Ranch Management Program at TCU from 1961-94 and recipient in 2005 of the National Golden Spur Award, the highest honor a rancher can receive. It is not, I think, well known that the father of this unfailingly courteous but rigorously demanding teacher of over 970 Ranch Management graduates made available his major library collection to help start the excellent library of the Amon Carter Museum.

Ron Flowers lecturing on church and state, his academic specialty.

ment, the honorary degree of Doctor of Science.

While I have mentioned several of my exceptional colleagues already and there are simply too many more impressive ones to name—all delightful, engaging, intellectually alive colleagues—I do want to mention the John R. Weatherly Emeritus Professor of Religion, my close friend and longtime racquetball partner, Ron Flowers, whose co-authored 1200-page fifth edition of *Religious Freedom and the Supreme Court* has been revised and updated with one co-author, Steven Green, a TCU Honors Program graduate. For many of my earlier years at TCU, I leaned on Jim Corder, a colleague generous with his eighteenth-century British courses, but Ron and I both arrived in 1966, and he has been a present help in times of trouble—and of joy—for all these years. We both have chaired the Faculty Senate and been privileged to work there with keen colleagues like Manny Reinecke, Geraldine Dominiak, the late Wayne Ludvigson, Sanoa Hensley—but I quickly run out of space. We share gratitude for our opportunity to work at TCU. I once requested Chancellor Tucker to write a note of encouragement to my younger brother Danny, dying of cancer in Lubbock Methodist Hospital. Here is the beginning of that letter, shown to me by my late brother: "Your brother and I work together at TCU." That sense of collegiality has been, for Ron and me, a hallmark of the academics at TCU during our more than forty-three years here. To have worked with Bill Tucker, and Libby Proffer, and Betsy Colquitt, and Rich Enos, and Ron—what a privilege. And Ron and I both appreciate, unabashedly, our colleagues, genuine colleagues, at this university. We treasure collegiality.

Of course, TCU has changed remarkably during my tenure here. In 1966, each young woman was issued a TCU official "Cues for Coeds,"

Moreover, he provided his son John duplicate copies of those books, helping to account for John's incredible knowledge of Western Americana. This truly modest but uncommonly gifted colleague held the Burnett Ranches Professorship, and TCU bestowed on him, at the May 2008 commence-

Yearbook 1986, pages 58-59.
Intensive study for ranchers.

stating shorts were not to be worn outside the dormitories. When "coeds" walked to the library they often wore raincoats over their shorts (so I heard) to skirt the rule. But two relatively recent *Skiff* headlines may suggest a somewhat different atmosphere on our campus: "Condom Committee Members Seeking Campus Recognition" (September 28, 1988) and "Alcohol Sales Ok'd Near Coliseum" (December 5, 2002). There are certainly many physical changes. Where I parked in 1966 and got a ticket is now covered by new dormitories (King, Carter, and others) with a new Brown-Lupton University Union at one end near Stadium Drive and a brand-new Scharbauer Hall just behind the newly renovated Reed Hall. My colleagues in the departments of Economics and Sociology, for example, reside now in Scharbauer, no longer having offices in portable buildings. Scharbauer sits near where the old Administration Auditorium originally sat, the site of many graduations when TCU moved from Waco to Fort Worth, and, sadly, one of the casualties of the recent expansion was the Faculty Center, a room

filled with invaluable history and good conversation. You have only to mention this sad loss to that extraordinary teacher/scholar and quintessential gentleman, Paul Boller—who found lunch and intellectual engagement there in the Faculty Center with colleagues from many disciplines to be one of the joys of his life—to realize how deeply disappointing this significant change has been for many of us.

Certainly a big change has taken place in how academics communicate on campus. From my office in Reed 221, long before e-mail, I used to tape letters in my window for my daughters Cynthia and Brenda in nearby Jarvis Dormitory to read, such as: "Dear Cynthia: Where is the hair dryer? Destitutely yours, Dad" and she replied from her dormitory corner window: "Dear Dad, Brenda has it. Love, Cindy." And on March 16, 1978, I found in my mailbox this "While You Were Out" telephone message from Phyllis Drake, English Department secretary: "Terri Stewart won't be in class today—has to go and get her marriage license; she's getting married Sat." Terri has long served

Yearbook 1986, page 143.
Celeste Palmer (psychology) shows
whom she thanks for her college
education as she waits in line outside
the coliseum. Placing tape on the top
of caps to form messages was popular
among many graduates.

as Executive Assistant in the TCU Athletics Department, and her children attended TCU. Now, I
correspond daily with my colleagues and students
by e-mail, if not Twitter and Facebook, and Tech-
nical Resources, the Koehler Center for Teaching
Excellence, and the Williams L. Adams Writing
Center stand by to help us all.

I had no key to Reed Hall for the first ten
years I taught in it, but my good friend and
colleague Professor Ted Klein of the Philosophy
Department informed me that the windows on the
porch of Reed were never locked. So I often
crawled through them on weekends to get to my
second floor office, my spouse's complaints that I
could "get shot by a TCU policeman" notwith-
standing. It was in Reed classroom 103 that I
discovered the "Reed Hall Flasher," who had
eluded TCU authorities for more than three years.
He stood, disheveled, peering through the blinds
at the Sadler/Reed mall area where my Major
British Writers students were sitting on the walls

taking a mid-class break during our three week
summer session course in May 1994. I chased the
famous flasher out of Reed, dashing through the
middle of my class sitting in the Sadler mall and
darting into Sadler Hall where a security officer
helped me catch him. I had had a quite different
memorable experience in Reed on April 8, 1992.
Following a discussion during the preceding class
meeting about the movie *Dead Poets Society,* I
entered classroom 314 to discover the entire honors freshman class, eleven students, standing
tightly packed on my large desk at the front of the
room addressing me, "O Captain, my Captain"
as they alluded to Robin Williams' portrayal of an
English teacher. This surprise was a pleasant one.

One revered TCU tradition, now sadly gone,
was the annual dinner honoring TCU retirees. You
could attend these formal affairs and honor retir-
ing colleagues, listening to the inspiring citations
read aloud which noted each retiree's accomplish-
ments and contributions to TCU life. I vividly
remember attending the "Candlelight Dinner"
held May 4, 1971, in the then recently renovated
Brown-Lupton Student Center. That evening, eight
faculty and staff members were honored, including Elmer Henson, Dean of Brite Divinity School,
and Lorraine Sherley, sans pink tennis shoes, who
had been a student and teacher at TCU for more
than fifty years. It was wondrous to hear their
citations.

The Creative Writing Awards have changed,
too. Beginning in 1939 with much leadership from
Mabel Major, who chaired the Creative Writing
Committee from 1947 to 1963, the annual Cre-
ative Writing Convocations attracted major writ-
ers like Robert Frost, Vachel Lindsay, Stephen
Spender, W. H. Auden, Isaac Bashevis Singer, and
Larry McMurtry. In 1975, I was shaking Robert
Penn Warren's hand when unreserved photogra-

Bob Frye with Pulitizer Prize-winning novelist and poet Robert Penn Warren on February 26, 1975, after Warren's Cecil B. Williams Lecture on "Democracy and Poetry." Photo by Linda Kaye, courtesy of Bob Frye.

pher Linda Kaye ordered, in her delightful but effective way, me and the two-time Pulitzer Prize winner and future first Poet Laureate of the United States to stop what we were doing and pose for a picture; we did. Now the Creative Writing Awards are held in the Kelly Center, a much smaller place than the old auditorium in what became Reed Hall or in Ed Landreth Auditorium. Yet the awards ceremony remains an important part of the TCU English Department, and I regularly encourage students to submit entries. In fact, I attended the annual event last week, and Grace Hughston, a business major from San Angelo who last spring was in my freshman seminar, Literary Culture of the American Southwest, won first prize in the AddRan Essay contest and got her essay published. I like to think that Mabel Major would have been pleased.

Although there is not space here to recognize properly the contributions of the many generous donors to TCU academics, I would be remiss if I did not pay tribute to the enormous contributions of the extraordinary philanthropists Cecil and Ida Green. In 1989, the Massachusetts Institute of Technology Press published Robert Shrock's book, *Cecil and Ida Green: Philanthropists Extraordinary,* describing their incredible gifts all over the world to support education, including Green College at Oxford University, England. At TCU the Greens endowed the Cecil H. and Ida Green Honors Chair, which enables renowned scholars from various disciplines to have limited-time appointments to our faculty called Visiting Green Professors. The holder of the first chair, Dr. Warner Rice of the University of Michigan, spent a full semester at TCU in 1971 teaching the first half of the survey of British literature and actively participating in the department. I sat in on Dr. Rice's class, learning along with the other students, and then had the rare privilege of succeeding him by teaching these same students the second half of the course in the spring of 1972. Subsequent Green Chair appointments for various periods of time have enabled students to learn from 365 of these distinguished professors between 1971 and 2009.

Among the other Green contributions to TCU are the Ida M. Green Fellowship Program supporting graduate students in PhD programs, substantial funding of the 1983 expansion of the Mary Couts Burnett Library (the Reading Room now bears their names), and the Cecil and Ida Green Distinguished Emeritus Tutor awards for various departments. My colleague Ron Flowers in Religion, for example, was a recent recipient of this generous award. When Dr. Green was honored in Washington, DC, September 20, 1987, by the National Academy of Sciences—he had been a founder of Texas Instruments—Chancellor William Tucker and his wife, Jean, attended. Commenting on the Greens on that occasion, Chancellor Tucker observed, "They are two of the most remarkable people on the face of the earth" (*TCU Daily Skiff,* October 6, 1987).

Before commenting briefly on the direction of academic programs in recent years, I want to call attention to a real success story: the TCU Press. Founded in 1966, the TCU Press has developed remarkably under the leadership of Dr. Judy Alter, Editor in 1982, Director 1987-2009. At Judy's retirement gathering in the fall of 2009, my longtime colleague and good friend Fred Erisman, TCU Emeritus Professor of English who held the Charles A. Lindbergh Chair in Aerospace History at the National Air and Space Museum, Smithsonian Institution, 2002-03, described the TCU Press as "one of the best university presses west of the Mississippi River." This is high commendation

indeed, for Dr. Erisman is invariably judicious in his praise.

Academic programs seem to be thriving, with Brite Divinity School offering study leading to the Doctor of Ministry degree in 1969, a Master of Theological Studies in 1988, and in 1997 the Doctor of Philosophy, for example. Although Professor Charles Sherer introduced courses in engineering in 1937 and there was a pre-professional program in engineering in the 1960s and 1970s, Emeritus Dean of Science and Engineering Michael McCracken tells me that in 1986-87 a committee considered the need for a department of engineering, Dr. Hal Nelson was hired from Arizona State University, and "engineering came on board" in 1991.

One of its most impressive professors, Dr. Ed Kolesar, whose daughter Lauren had been in my English class, died recently; he was the Moncrief Professor of Engineering. Meanwhile, the Department of Music has become the School of Music, and Art is now the Department of Art and Art History with, for example, a Master of Arts in Art History. The College of Education now has several institutes, such as the Andrews Institute of Mathematics & Science Education, and it now offers the PhD in Educational Studies: Science.

There are more than fifty endowed chairs, many in the Neeley School of Business which continues to climb higher in national rankings and offers the distinctive Neeley Fellows Program. Harris College has a new Doctor of Nursing Practice degree, and AddRan has a brand new building, Scharbauer, to house its offices and several of its fifteen departments, a state-of-the-art webpage, and new mission and vision statements to help it implement new programs and emphases such as the English Department's writing major. Students and faculty as well find encouraging and helpful the work of the Adams Center for Writing. With all these academic possibilities, and with more emphasis on a residential TCU student body to fill all those new dormitories, the sign I saw in 1977 outside of Trinity College, Cambridge University, England, seems true: "People live and study here."

To provide personal impressions of academics at TCU during its 100 years on the Fort Worth campus—well, a larger canvas is needed. But I will stop here and draw on an experience, leaving you with an impression which I hope you may find useful.

In 1992, it was my privilege to direct the junior honors project of Elizabeth Lunday. She had won the AddRan Essay Award in the 1990 TCU Creative Writing Contest for a paper she had written for my honors section of freshman English, and in 1992 she won not only the Lorraine Sherley Prize but also the Woman's Wednesday Club Merit Award for the junior English major with the most "distinguished academic achievement." In our conference on Friday, April 3, I raised several questions with Elizabeth about some feminist positions. I noted I had learned considerable from a *College English* essay quoting Carol Gilligan, who argues in her book *In a Different Voice* for a conception of morality "concerned with the activity of care [which] centers moral development around the understanding of responsibility and relationships," not rights and rules. On Monday, April 6, I received a nine-page printed letter, not assigned, from Elizabeth, dated April 4, which opens with these paragraphs:

> *Once again you have done the unspeakable—you have made me think. Gee, thanks a lot.*
>
> *Over the past few years, I've done a great deal of reading about feminism, women's issues, etc. I've never set those*

thoughts down before or tried to organize them.

In talking to you about the article on feminist criticism and the Gilligan book (which keeps popping up in unexpected places), I decided to explain the thoughts which I've put under the "feminist" label. I want to share these thoughts with you not only because I like telling people what I think but also because I know this is a subject you have thought about.

Perhaps between the two of us, we can discover something true.

This sense of discovering, together—student with faculty, faculty with student—is the impression I hope to leave with you of TCU academics during the 100 years since the move from Waco to Fort Worth. It comes close to what England's Poet Laureate John Masefield once wrote about the nature of a university: "There are few earthly things more beautiful than a university, a place where those who hate ignorance may strive to know, where those who perceive truth may strive to [help] others see."

....

BOB J. FRYE
Emeritus Professor of English

4

TCU, FORT WORTH, AND THE ARTS

RON TYLER

Ballet students' annual spring performance, 2004. In 1949, TCU became the first university in the nation to offer a BFA in ballet. The School of Ballet and Modern Dance has since developed an indisputable reputation as one of the finest programs in the nation, providing talented young dancers with world-class instruction.

My memory of the fine arts while I was a student at TCU is how seamlessly they blended into campus life, whether a Cliburn competition or symphony performance at Ed Landreth, a Little Theater production, or the European old masters of Velma and Kay Kimbell that hung in various campus buildings before the Kimbell Art Museum opened.

And, while I did not realize it at the time, the works of art blended equally well with the city. By then, of course, the ties between town and gown had been well established by generations of TCU alumni who had graduated into the community, their world enlarged by on-campus concerts and exhibitions as well as formal classes. Some had even taken a major in what is now the College of Fine Arts and had assumed positions in business and cultural organizations—the symphony, opera, ballet, theater, and museums.

The fine arts have been a part of campus life at TCU since the early days at Thorp Spring when art and music first became a part of the formal curriculum. By the time TCU moved to Fort Worth in 1910, the College of Music and schools of Oratory and Painting and Drawing offered training to students. Today the College of Fine Arts provides students with courses in art and art history, classical and contemporary dance, music, theatre, design, merchandising, and textiles, and has grown to include more than nine hundred students majoring in seventeen fields and twenty-seven concentrations.

Historically, universities have been seen as "cities set on a hill," a part of the global rather than the local community, pursuing universal truths. The student experience can be something of a cocoon, encouraging communing with the ancients or trying to envision the future. However,

Yearbook 1925, page 163.
TCU 1925 Band.

twenty-first century pressures and values have led TCU to seek nearby opportunities to expand educational experiences and to enrich the larger society, and each of the programs in the College of Fine Arts reaches into the community in significant ways.

The most obvious connection lies in the training of students who move directly into the economy, whether it be as performer, educator, participant, audience member, or board member and supporter of the arts. Scott Sullivan, Dean of the College of Fine Arts, noted that "We help create the leaders and the audiences for the arts in Fort Worth." This reflects the theories of economist Richard Florida, who says that creative people are needed to build humane, sustainable cities and to help us lead more fulfilling lives. He reports that in 1910, about the time TCU moved to Fort Worth, fewer than 10 percent of American work-

ers were engaged in what he calls creative work—artists, musicians, designers, scientists, engineers. The other 90 percent were working on farms or in factories, earning a living from the land and their physical labor; this percentage was probably higher in Texas. But in the twenty-first century, farmers make up only about 10 percent of the population, and more than one-third of the workforce earns its living from creative undertakings. Florida considers the presence of a major university a necessary part of creating a "people climate," and, as a nurturer of creativity, innovation, and entertainment, the TCU College of Fine Arts has proven to be an important cultural as well as economic stimulus for the community.

The Van Cliburn Foundation's quadrennial International Piano Competition, for example, has become one of the staples of the community, with regular concerts and children's educational pro-

*Yearbook 1975, page 362.
Symphony Orchestra. The
TCU Symphony Orchestra is
composed of about sixty
players, most who are majors
and minors in music. How-
ever, some of its members
come from other depart-
ments. Orchestra concerts,
open to the public without
charge, were given approximately once a month.*

grams throughout the year. The first Cliburn piano competition was held at TCU in 1962, only four years after the twenty-three-year-old pianist made history with his victory at the first International Tchaikovsky Competition in Moscow on April 14, 1958. Inspired by his extraordinary accomplishment, a group of Fort Worth music teachers and private citizens organized and established the Van Cliburn Foundation and International Piano Competition.

A few years later, in 1972, a young TCU graduate who had recently returned from study at the Conservatoire Royal de Musique in Brussels became Musical Director and Conductor of the Fort Worth Symphony Orchestra. John Giordano served in that capacity for twenty-seven years and at the same time was a member of the jury for the Van Cliburn International Piano Competition, chairing the jury for a number of years. Today Giordano teaches student musicians at TCU in addition to his other undertakings.

The Cliburn Competition is now held at Bass Performance Hall, but the university continues to serve as one of two concert halls in the United States where auditions for the competition are held. The thirteenth competition took place in 2009 with Ang Li, a Canadian enrolled in the Artist Diploma Program at TCU, as one of the competitors.

The Cliburn Competition has also provided other benefits for the university, both locally and internationally, and has helped TCU build a respected piano program. The redoubtable Madame Lili Kraus came to Fort Worth as a juror for the inaugural competition, then combined her worldwide performing career with a position as artist-in residence at TCU for the next decade and a half. Two Cliburn Competition gold medal winners have since filled the artist-in-residence chair: Steven De Groote, the 1977 winner, and now Brazilian José Feghali, the 1985 winner.

Another collaborative program between the university, the Van Cliburn Foundation, and the Fort Worth Symphony is Piano Texas International Academy and Festival, begun in 1981 by Hungarian-born pianist Tamás Ungár, a member of the piano faculty. Ungár created the program to provide advanced educational opportunities for outstanding international pre-college and college piano students, piano teachers, and adult amateurs. Piano Texas provides intense training from members of the world's most famous conservatories on the TCU campus and has evolved into an international music festival where, according to *Southern Living*, each June Fort Worth becomes "Piano Town U.S.A." as the visiting artists provide local audiences with a wonderful opportunity to hear world-class solo, concerto, and chamber music concerts. Appropriately enough, TCU was designated as the first all-Steinway school in Texas.

One summer event that has developed a strong town and gown following is the Mimir Chamber Music Festival. Named for the Norse god of wisdom, the festival features outstanding artists from the world's leading orchestras and music schools and has become the premier festival in the South Central United States dedicated exclusively to the study and performance of chamber music. Throughout the two-week summer festival, guest artists hold master classes for aspiring pre-professional musicians. In the evenings, guest musicians present a series of exciting musical performances for the public. In 2009, guest artists included members of the Chicago Symphony and Cleveland Orchestra as well as winners of the Van Cliburn and Leeds International Piano competi-

tions and outstanding TCU faculty.

The Center for Latin American Music at TCU, in conjunction with the Fort Worth Symphony Orchestra, presented its first biennial Latin American Music Festival in the spring of 1998, hosting performances and lectures by artists and composers. The center emphasizes the performance, recording, and dissemination of music of Latin American composers by collecting and cataloging both published and unpublished music as well as serving as a liaison to promote commissions of new works. The festival is a unique opportunity for Texas audiences to hear composers and talent from South America and the Caribbean performing classical music rarely heard in the United States.

Opera students have a chance to perform in two campus productions each year in Ed Landreth Auditorium as well as with the Fort Worth Opera. The TCU Opera Studio was established with a TCU Vision in Action grant in the summer of 2007, coinciding with the Fort Worth Opera's change to festival format. The Opera Studio has a relationship with the Fort Worth Opera that offers students the opportunity to perform with the Opera Chorus, in shared productions in the Young Artist Program, and in master classes with Fort Worth Opera artists and to receive professional advice from FWO professionals. The Opera Studio continues under the guidance of Associate Professor Richard Estes, the institute director. Legendary mezzo soprano Marilyn Horne presented a series of master classes to twelve TCU voice students in 2009.

The same kind of collaboration distinguishes the art and art history programs, with TCU faculty and graduates working in museums and galleries throughout the region. The fine arts program received a huge boost in 1982, when

RIGHT
Moments after his Gold Medal winning performance in the 1985 Van Cliburn International Piano Competition, José Feghali is flooded with congratulations. The 1985 competition was held in TCU's Ed Landreth Auditorium. Courtesy, Fort Worth Star-Telegram Collection, Special Collections, *The University of Texas at Arlington Library, Arlington, Texas.*

BOTTOM RIGHT
Studio space for aspiring young artists at TCU's Waco campus, 1911.

Yearbook 1995, page 233. Members of SAICA perform in the fashion show that concluded Experience Asia, a banquet that raised about $9,000 to aid Mother Teresa's work in Asia.

where he provided graphic and bold illustrations for *Time, National Geographic, National Lampoon, Playboy,* and many commercial accounts, including the packaging for the enormously popular video game *Doom.* He taught illustration as an adjunct professor at TCU for thirty-five years, until his death in 2009, and was known to his friends and students as the "Godfather of Dallas Illustration," because his arrival helped inspire what many now see as a golden age of illustration and design in the North Texas area.

The Exhibition Hall of the Moudy has been the scene of a number of notable exhibitions, not the least of which was a 1985 exhibition, organized by Ronald Watson, himself an artist and Chair of the Department of Art and Art History, of fifty years of Fort Worth artist Bror Utter's paintings and prints. The Moudy space has been hosting the annual "Art in the Metroplex" exhibition for the past twenty-seven years. The 2009 show included thirty pieces by twenty-two artists.

Recently, as a part of TCU's Vision in Action initiative, the university established Fort Worth Contemporary Arts to exhibit challenging work by local, national, and international artists. The TCU Department of Art and Art History has ambitious plans to make Fort Worth Contemporary Arts a significant cultural resource that will not only allow students to gain knowledge of the practices and issues related to exhibition organization, but also invigorate North Texas with exposure to cutting-edge contemporary art.

The Department of Design, Merchandising and Textiles is especially connected to the community because students are required to do extensive internships in local and regional businesses. Students can prepare for careers in interior design or any aspect of merchandising. The Center for Lighting Education, established in 1998, provides the unusual opportunity for students to work with

Kevin Roche John Dinkeloo and Associates designed the J. M. Moudy Visual Arts and Communication Building as the new home for fine arts and communications. At the same time, the program was growing and adding new faculty. Professor Mark Thistlethwaite, who holds the Kay and Velma Kimbell Chair of Art History, arrived at TCU in 1977 and has trained dozens of students who teach art and art history and work in museums around the country, including the Amon Carter Museum, the Kimbell Art Museum, and the Modern Art Museum of Fort Worth. In addition, he serves on the board of the Modern and on the Visiting Committee of the Carter, and has served as chair of the Fort Worth Art Commission.

Also arriving in the 1970s was Don Ivan Punchatz, who established a studio in Arlington,

Yearbook 1968, page 75. TCU and Fort Worth Arts merge.

professionals in the field to mock up retail design sets to understand the impact of lighting. Energy efficiency, as well as the use of color, angles, and intensities to create different moods, is emphasized.

The TCU Department of Theatre presented its first season in 1945-46. Since that time it has trained performers for the local and national stage, including the many amateur and professional companies in the North Texas area. One of the early graduates of the program was Bill Garber, who for many years was director of the Fort Worth Community Theater. The work of Garber and other veterans of the TCU program helped inspire many of the spin-offs in today's vibrant local theater scene such as Circle Theatre (which derives its name from its original home on Bluebonnet Circle, near TCU), Hip Pocket Theatre, the Trin-

ity Shakespeare Festival, Kids Who Care, Amphibian Stage Productions (founded in 2000 by three alumni of the TCU Department of Theatre), Texas Nonprofit Theatres, Inc., the American Association of Community Theatre, Stage West, and many others. Johnny and Diane Simons, two of the three founders of Hip Pocket Theatre in 1976, graduated from the TCU theatre program, as did Jim Covault, the artistic director of Stage West, who joined the company during its first season in 1979. Like other companies, Stage West and Circle Theatre have done several co-productions with the TCU Theatre Department. Harry B. Parker, Chair of the Department of Theatre and Managing Director of the Trinity Shakespeare Festival, also did his undergraduate work at TCU.

One of the university's most famous alumni is Betty Lynn Buckley, winner of the Miss Fort

Yearbook 1979, page 79. Drama.

Worth pageant and a runner-up for Miss Texas. I first realized that Betty was headed toward a distinguished career as I was walking across campus with my future wife one cold morning and saw Betty being interviewed by CBS television in front of Dave Reed Hall. On a subsequent trip to New York, I saw posters for her 1969 Broadway debut in *1776*. She went on to win a Tony Award for her performance as Grizabella in Andrew Lloyd Webber's *Cats*. Today Betty teaches classes and workshops in Fort Worth and sponsors the Betty Lynn Buckley Awards Honoring Excellence in High School Musical Theatre as she continues her performing career.

In 1949, TCU became the first college in the country to offer a Bachelor of Fine Arts degree in ballet. In 1964, Fernando Schaffenburg, a veteran of the American Ballet Theatre and of Broadway, joined the department and built a graduate program with a national reputation. In the mid-1960s, he started the Fort Worth Ballet and became its director as well. The Fort Worth Ballet evolved into today's Texas Ballet Theater, performing in both Fort Worth and Dallas, with internationally known Ben Stevenson as artistic director, who also teaches in the Department of Ballet and Modern Dance. The school regularly offers students opportunities to perform internationally, most recently in Mexico and Japan, and celebrated its sixtieth anniversary in 2009.

The importance of a reciprocal relationship between a university and its community cannot be underestimated, and in their century of coexistence, TCU and Fort Worth have come to define one another and to create an electric cultural arts center on the West side of the Metroplex.

RON TYLER, *TCU, MA 1966; PhD 1968*
Former Director, Amon Carter Museum

5

FORT WORTH AND TCU'S CAMPUS LIFE

VICKI VINSON CANTWELL

"Hail all hail, TCU
Memories Sweet, Comrades True
Light of Faith, Follow Through
Praise to Thee, TCU."

Yearbook 1979, page 246.

The chimes of Robert Carr Chapel play the Alma Mater of Texas Christian University every afternoon at five o'clock. Whenever I hear these bells, I immediately smile, as the sound brings back "memories sweet" of my time at TCU. I treasure my memories and my many "comrades true." I may have graduated from TCU three decades ago in May 1978, but it seems like yesterday. I remember vividly the Sunday morning after graduation when the security guard came into the Delta Delta Delta sorority house to tell my girlfriends and me that we had to leave; he had to lock up for summer. As exhilarated as I was to start the next chapter of life, leaving was bittersweet. We had shared an amazing four years together and stood on the hot asphalt parking lot, crying, and hugging.

My experiences were not an exception; they were probably typical of most. There are certain experiences that every college student has in common, including the excitement of receiving your letter of acceptance. Mine arrived in early spring of 1974. I ran across it recently and laughed that I had kept my acceptance letter but very few grade reports. It is "typed," not laser printed, probably on a Smith-Corona (remember those?), and quite faint. The paper may have faded, but my memories certainly haven't. The entire world had just opened up to me, a small-town Texas girl off to the big city—Fort Worth. It was one hour and a world away from Bridgeport, Texas. I would be taking college classes, living in a dormitory, going

What Does It Take To Be A Horned Frog?

"Pride, or more specific, Purple Pride"

— James Link

Yearbook 1986, page 59. Quote.

to football games, joining a sorority, and making new friends. I had big dreams and expectations; I was never disappointed.

College and campus living affords every student a unique opportunity through personal challenges that form who you become. Campus life is a dialogue composed of the interaction of students with students and students with faculty and staff. Life on a university campus provides a unique opportunity to create yourself in a community. TCU is a student-friendly campus, perhaps more so today than ever, and the university has always had clear goals for its role in the student's life: to provide for the health, safety, social, and academic success of each of its students.

Campus life revolves around the academic calendar: dates to move in, first day of class, football schedule, papers due, basketball schedule, road trips to games or other schools to visit friends or hometown-honeys (HTH), trips home to see parents and do laundry. Of course, the academic calendar and student policies have evolved from

the first ones written by the Clarks in the school catalog of 1883-1884; they were strict: two holidays and no one went home before Christmas. In other ways the Clarks were quite progressive. In September 1873, when AddRan Male and Female Academy opened with thirteen students in Thorp Spring, forty miles southwest of Fort Worth, it was considered quite progressive for welcoming female students. The total enrollment for fall 2009 was 8,696, students comprising 7,471 undergraduates and 1,225 graduate students. That year marked the largest incoming freshman class in history, with an enrollment of over 1,800. When the campus was relocated to its current location, it seemed a protective world away from downtown Fort Worth. Today the five miles are filled with cultural diversity, businesses that provide internships and employment, and great entertainment. The "big small-town" feel of Fort Worth, with its cultural institutions and welcoming downtown, enhances the experience of TCU students.

The ten decades of life on the campus of TCU have seen two World Wars, the Korean War, Vietnam, the Gulf War, and the War on Terror. Each of these conflicts have affected the student body in unique ways and have sometimes brought struggles of their own onto campus. In the late 1960s and early 1970s, college campuses across the country experienced antagonism between administration and student body. The serene campus of TCU was no exception; it had student demonstrations and even streakers. But as Mark Mourer wrote in his *TCU Magazine* article from winter 2009, the administration chose to "give and take" by allowing Jerry Garcia and the Grateful Dead to perform in Daniel-Meyer Coliseum on November 14, 1971. A year earlier when Jefferson Airplane came to campus, students were so unruly that the administration banned rock concerts.

RIGHT
Yearbook 1986, page 162. Tom Brown room of 209, home of Barry Lewis and Todd Camp, was noted as one of the more fascinating rooms on campus due to the high volume of unusual items on display. Although many tried to emulate the decor, one neighbor commented that "Most of it needs to be burned."

BOTTOM RIGHT
Yearbook 1979, page 64. Dorm life.

Yearbook 1961, page 9.

the campus. None, though, resonated in music and cultural history as strongly as the Dead.

Each generation of Horned Frogs looks back at the campus with its own unique mental images: the serenity of Robert Carr Chapel or Amon G. Carter Stadium, without the upper tier for earlier generations, and now the John S. Justin Athletic Center in the south end zone. In the mid-1960s, Worth Hills saw construction of the fraternity and sorority houses. Of course, whether you lived on the main campus or in the Greek section, you were still living with curfews and had to sign out on weekends when you were going home. These policies remained in force through the early 1970s.

Frog Fountain holds sentimental value for me, but it didn't come to campus until 1969. For students today, the tower of the Brown-Lupton University Union, which glows purple at night, is an iconic image of the campus. As the face of the campus grew and changed, so did various student organizations. The *TCU Daily Skiff* has been serving the TCU community since 1902, and whether picked up in hard copy from stands all over campus or read electronically, it has been a welcome constant. Student government also remains integral to TCU. Since 1914, the mission of the Student Government Association has been to represent the collective voice of the student body while encompassing the spirit of the TCU community through service, programming, and legislation. Over the decades, Programming Council, or its related entities, have brought interesting speakers, films, and performers to campus, and the TCU Pep Cabinet created the Horned Frog mascot, Addy, the All-American Frog, in 1949.

The TCU Band was first formed in 1904, comprised of TCU students and members of the Fort Worth community. When the 1910 fire spread through the Main Building on the campus

However, the administration, and particularly Libby Proffer, Director of Student Services, gave the students a second chance. Rock music historians say that the TCU performance was seminal to the Grateful Dead's becoming a touring band. A few years later, in the mid-1970s, Michael Martin Murphey played Daniel-Meyer Coliseum and, recently, Pat Green, among others, also entertained

RIGHT
Yearbook 1969, page 36.

FAR RIGHT
Yearbook 1986, page 3.
Frog Fountain continues the
time-honored tradition of
playing host to students
having birthdays.

of TCU in Waco, the music department lost nine upright pianos, one grand piano, a pipe organ, W. T. Hamner's (director of the TCU Glee Club) music library, and every classroom on campus. The need to relocate classes required every square inch of the remaining buildings, including the music rooms, so the band would lay dormant while TCU found a new home. A year later, in 1911, B. A. Kirkpatrick, a TCU medical student and brother of TCU's first band director Charles Kirkpatrick, gathered a group of medical students and undergrads to form a group for the sole purpose   of playing at the cornerstone-laying ceremony for the new administration building (now called Reed Hall). Years later Claude Sammis was named Chairman of the Music Department, orchestra director, and then band director. He wrote the TCU Fight Song in 1928, and by that time the band had grown to forty-one members and traveled with the football team to each away game. The TCU band website gives a wonderful chronological   history of the band and the amazing directors who have led it. Among the stories told is that of Leon Breeden from 1944–1949:

[The] band was made up largely of veterans of WWII who were nearly impossible to control. One year, after the Fort Worth Fat Stock Show Parade, the band guys somehow acquired a big white horse. They then proceeded to ride the horse through the old Administration Building marching behind it and jamming to "Onward Christian Soldiers." Another year the football team and band went by train to Kansas City for the University of Kansas game. A large rain storm came just after the game had started. Part of the band's show that day was to spell out "HELLO" on the field. The drum major took the band behind the stadium during the 2nd quarter and changed the show just slightly. First they spelled "O HELL", and then the "O" ran to the other end of the formation spelling "HELLO."

Dr. Lorraine Sherley, who taught English at TCU from 1927-1971, founded and lovingly directed the Bryson Literary Club. Campus Alumni Board (CAB), now the Student Foundation, brought

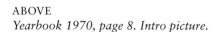

ABOVE
Yearbook 1970, page 8. Intro picture.

UPPER RIGHT
Yearbook 1986, page 2. During the Activities Carnival of Howdy Week, the Career Center borrows an idea from the comic strip "Peanuts" to inform students of their service.

LOWER RIGHT
Yearbook 1943, page 83. Through these portals...

RIGHT
*Yearbook 1964, page 232.
Pi Beta Phi's homecoming
float won second place in
the class "B" division.*

FAR RIGHT
*Yearbook 1969, page 57.
More scenes from '68
Homecoming: floats,
females, football, and fun.*

students together with alumni throughout the year, but particularly at Homecoming. Homecoming is always a special time of the year, but in 1976 it was a bit unusual. The Homecoming Committee had not expected the snowfall North Texas received overnight on Friday. The Homecoming parade and other festivities were cancelled, but the game against the University of Texas was played, *after* the field was snowplowed.

Student life has never been only about academics. As far back as May 1918, the *TCU Daily Skiff* reported on Spring Festival, later in the 1920s also referred to as the Jubilee Pageant, the First Pageant of May, or May Fête. Usually held in the athletic stadium, the ode to spring included coronation ceremonies of the royal princesses and others, complete with trumpeters as well as athletic competitions, musical presentations, and folk

dancing. In 1941, the *Skiff* reported that there were at least 225 performers. This tradition continued until the U.S. entered World War II, which brought dramatic changes to the demographics of the student body. A few years later this tradition was reinvented as Frog Follies and has been reinvented many times over in the intervening decades.

After World War II, life on campus settled down as veterans returned to school. Students create traditions and those traditions evolve with generations; the post-war Baby Boomers witnessed new traditions in Ranch Week and the Singing Seminarians. Over the decades the demographics of the student body have also seen change. In 1938, students of other faiths outnumbered Disciples of Christ students. As a result of national politics, the university was racially integrated in

Yearbook 1990, page 114.

ganizations. The Greek model stands for academic achievement, strong character, and service to the fraternity, the university, and the community. The Greek system at TCU is particularly successful at mentoring freshmen and encouraging leadership and service, both on campus and off.

Members of my chapter, Delta Delta Delta, have sold programs at the football games for over forty-five years. All the money is designated for scholarships for undergraduate women at TCU. Selling programs is quite an honor and actually great fun. You are able to be in the midst of the energy and excitement of a football game. The first time I sold programs, I was assigned to the northwest corner of the stadium, not far from the elevator to the press box and chancellor's suite. I wasn't smart enough at the time to appreciate meeting the influential people who bought programs from me and proceeded upstairs to the chancellor's and the athletic director's boxes. Little did I know that the university provided them with programs, but out of generosity most of these guests chose to buy a program and support our philanthropy. Of all these Horned Frog fans, one stood out above the others. He was a slight, elderly man, but he had a strong presence, a nice smile, and always a warm hello. He graciously asked to buy a program, gave me his money, but said to give the program to someone else because he knew the players by heart. I was quite taken aback and just said, "Thank you very much, sir." Fortunately, a sorority advisor, who happened to work in the chancellor's office, had watched this and asked if I knew who the man was. "No, ma'am," I replied. "That was Davey O'Brien!" What a treat. Mr. O'Brien, a legend to all fans of college football and particularly for Horned Frog fans, passed away in the football season of 1977, my senior year. I was honored to have met him.

1964 and the student body now includes a diverse student population. One of the biggest changes in student life at Texas Christian University came in 1955 when the first fraternity chapter was established. Declining enrollment in the early 1950s prompted the administration to consider bringing Greeks to campus. North Texas State University in Denton and Texas Tech in Lubbock had recently established fraternities and sororities. Despite some rather heated debates, protests, and a blue jean-clad effigy hung from a tree, the Board of Trustees approved adding Greek organizations in September 1954. Fifty years and thousands of members later, the Greek community thrives and today represents membership in as many as twenty-six national chapters and three local or-

RIGHT
*Yearbook 1967, page 364.
BSU longhorn-eating Horned
Frog wins the grand prize in
the float competition.*

BOTTOM RIGHT
Yearbook 1979, page 246.

ABOVE TOP
Yearbook 1990, page 34.
4th Annual TCU Frog Fest.

ABOVE BOTTOM
Cheerleaders unfurl the flag before
the 1994 Homecoming game.
Courtesy TCU Communications.

RIGHT
Yearbook 1961, page 110.
Lesson number one: One should
never try to attract attention during
rush by sticking her tongue out to
members.

Mr. O'Brien would have loved sitting in the stands in 2009 when the TCU Horned Frogs completed their first undefeated season since 1938, the year he led them to a national championship.

There were other great sports traditions—intramural ones—on campus. You've never seen competition until you have seen a Tri Delta–Kappa flag football game. *ESPN College Game-Day*, where were you? We were dogged competitors on the field and great friends off. Do keep in mind that on some occasions, we all weren't always perfect ladies, but we did have style. A good friend and classmate of mine, Mary Bailey, recounts a wonderful tale about how she and a few sisters replaced her sorority's chapter composites with those of a fraternity. One Friday night they loaded her car with old composites from the 1950s, sneaked into each of the fraternity houses, removed their current composite from the wall, and replaced it with one of the 1950 composites. Upon returning to the sorority house with their bounty, they hung the current composites in the hallway upstairs. The actives preferred the frat boys to their 1950s sisters. Their alum advisors, however, did not agree and insisted on correcting the switch, but the frat boys weren't too keen on doing so. Alas, to the chagrin of all, the advisors prevailed.

While some of my friends were redecorating chapter rooms, others were decorating each other's cars. One TCU coed was nicknamed Marshmallow because she was a beautiful blonde

ABOVE
Yearbook 1963, page 74.
"I think there is enough flour here for everybody. I don't know about those spoons, though."

ABOVE RIGHT
Yearbook 1979, page 48.
Sorority sack races.

with a pale peaches-and-cream complexion. But beneath that beautiful Renaissance façade, she was quite the mischievous prankster. Marshmallow regretted that her roommate left every Friday morning to drive to Austin to visit her HTH at UT. Marshmallow decided to make it a little harder for her. I can't admit or believe that we left our cars unlocked most of the time back then, but we did, since there were no CD players, GPS, or iPhone docks to steal. That enabled Marshmallow to easily access her roommate's car. She wadded up enough newspaper to completely fill the car. When her roommate came back from her Friday morning exam anxious to hit the road for Austin, she was confronted with a car she was unable to get into.

Of course, one good turn always deserves another, so on Sunday when the roommate returned from Austin, she left Marshmallow a present on her car. While driving back from Austin, the roommate bought bags and bags of marshmallows. After Marshmallow had gone to bed, the roommate went to the parking lot in front of the sorority house and completely dotted her car with, yes, marshmallows. It was a polka-dot delight.

Licking a marshmallow and sticking it to glass makes marshmallows like concrete, and substantial effort was required for Marshmallow to clean her windshield.

We weren't always playing jokes on each other. We were service minded also. All sororities and fraternities have their philanthropic allegiances and service projects to fund them. Two annual events that were a great tradition were Sigma Chi Derby Day and Phi Kap Man Day. For as many students as have attended TCU, there are three times that number of stories from these and similar events, such as the great "Gravy Train Sip and Slide" competition. Perhaps enough said.

Terminology used on campus today, as opposed to my mid-1970s day, is quite different. We no longer have the Student Center, but the BLUU, the Brown-Lupton University Union. Today, there is Greek recruitment, not rush, and new members, not pledges. Merely semantics. Otherwise, campus life for today's first-year student is not dramatically different from mine in 1974 or that of any incoming class. Many of them will have potluck roommates who turn out to be friends for life. Some will quickly discover that their study

ABOVE
Yearbook 1995, page 259.
After a performance at the Fall 1994
Minority Student Welcome Program.
Delta Sigma Theta members pause
outside the Brown-Lupton Student
Center.

ABOVE RIGHT
Yearbook 1986, page 4.
The divestment movement, aimed at
pressuring the South African govern-
ment to abandon apartheid, did not
escape the TCU campus. This rally
was planned for Students for a Dem-
ocratic South Africa to coincide with
a Board of Trustees meeting in
March.

habits and time management skills need some finessing. Others will gain the freshman fifteen, pounds, that is. This has always been easy to do, even without the soft serve ice cream machine at the Main or in the BLUU. But today, you can go to the Recreation Center, the enlarged version of the Rickel Center, and do some wall climbing or run on the treadmill at 6:00 AM to work off those calories. While many, if not most, of the buildings we knew have moved or been modified or retooled, their roles in the lives of the student body remain much the same.

A contagious energy permeates the TCU campus today. Walk into the Mary Couts Burnett Library on a Sunday afternoon before finals and see that every seat is filled with young (they look *very* young) people with their figurative eyes on the end of the semester, finals, Christmas, and a BCS bowl game. Almost every student wears something purple or something that says TCU.

The recurring theme of "some things change but most of them do not" comes back to us here—consider the library. Will you ever forget the smell of the books, the periodicals, or the stale coffee in the vending machines? Ah, but now we come to the changes. Remember the card catalogue—all those file drawers we used to flip through trying to find the one book that would spell out all of the answers? They aren't there. I did find one cabinet which had been moved to help create a barrier between the Reading Room and the new coffee/snacks area called Bistro Burnett, but the drawers were empty. In their place are many computers with access to the TCU library system. I'm sure computers are far more efficient, but I miss catalogue cards.

When I was at TCU, the concept of a computer was vague. There were a few people I knew who were taking a class called database management, I think. You could easily identify them be-

ABOVE
Yearbook 1969, page 254.
TCU's Yacht Club hosts
"nautical but nice" afternoon
outings.

ABOVE RIGHT
Yearbook 1970, page 18.
Rallies.

cause they would be carrying stacks of punch cards. We also didn't have microwaves or answering machines in our rooms. I was my roommate's answering machine, and she was mine. We actually survived without cell phones, voice mail, and e-mail. So, many things change: computers instead of card files, bistro coffee in the front room of the library, and drinks and snacks allowed in the Reading Room. Papers are written on laptops rather than legal pads or spiral notebooks. But the students haven't changed. They are still worried about finishing their papers in time, getting good grades, and passing accounting. Some things never change.

I hope that a few of these current students have found a favorite sanctuary of mine, the Music Library in Ed Landreth. The Music Library is a place of refuge where you can sit in a quiet room with great headsets and listen to anything you want. I asked to hear something new every time I went until the librarian recommended Brahms' four symphonies. Amazing. For the next two weeks we compared different versions until it was clear, beyond question, that the best performance was that of George Szell conducting the Cleveland Orchestra. Listen to it sometime.

The next time you are on campus, listen for the bells of Robert Carr Chapel playing the alma mater. Remember walking across campus on a beautiful day or think about those great spots just off campus that provided such comfort . . . comfort food, that is: Carlson's, home of the Bacon Burger; Merry-Go-Round; Mr. Beef; Caro's on Bluebonnet Circle (yes, near the Oui Lounge); and the 1849 Village. Do you remember O'Leary's Ice Cream Parlor? Did you ever drive over to College Street late in the evening, when you were studying very hard or writing a paper and decide you really needed a Lone Star Donut? If you waited late enough, they were really cheap. If donuts

Yearbook 1963, page 69. The bloodless revolution was a success. The library demonstrators had made their points. And the administration's cries of "too expensive" and "you wouldn't use the library anyway if it were open Sundays" broke down. Now the library is open Sundays. Just like the libraries at every other university in the Southwestern Conference. The revolt was won. "It's not as hard as it looks."

ABOVE
Yearbook 1979, page 183.
Delta Sigma Theta.

ABOVE RIGHT
Yearbook 1949, page 290.
The Yacht Club is the newest
and fastest growing on the
campus. Its purpose is to
promote freedom of the seas
at TCU and to orient nautical
(but nice) lines. As yet the
organization has no vessels,
but plans are being made to
set aside each year a portion
of the club's funds for invest-
ment made at two cent inter-
est. The resulting sum will be
used to buy a yacht. This will
be in 1982.

weren't bad enough, we would drive down University to the Ol' South Pancake House for omelets and pancakes. Sometimes you have to feed the mind with something in the stomach.

I would be remiss if I didn't acknowledge how many great evenings were had at Spencer's Corner or many other live music venues. I have great memories of spending evenings with girlfriends listening to a group of SAEs who had a fabulous fifties band, Phil Alpha and the Mystics. Oh, and the Stables. There were plenty of places to go in Fort Worth for fun, and some of them never change—Joe T. Garcia's, for example.

How grateful I am that Texas Christian University is a part of my life. Everyone has his or her own wonderful memories and tales. Take a moment to imagine the resonant chimes of Robert Carr Chapel and remember your memories sweet and comrades true.

VICKI VINSON CANTWELL, *Class of 1978*

6

THE TCU CAMPUS:
THEN AND NOW

MIKE MULLINS

Frog Fountain, a gift from the H. H. Phillips Family, arrived on campus in 1969. Its majestic purple glow calls to mind fond memories of student life for generations of Horned Frogs. Today the fountain is the centerpiece of TCU's campus commons, a housing community for upperclassmen constructed in 2008. Courtesy TCU Communications.

It was the fall of 1965, and I'd been accepted to the only university to which I'd applied. My first impression of the almost 250-acre TCU campus two years earlier was that the school colors should have been yellow and red. The grass—and there was a lot of it—was yellow; the buildings were yellow; the roofs were red. Though big and beautiful trees on either side of University Drive provided some green and shady relief, the prairie origins of the campus, circa 1910, complete with horned toads and coyotes, didn't seem all that distant. Fort Worth's slogan, "Where the West Begins," still had relevance.

As for the rest of the sprawling TCU landscape, the vast majority of its trees, tough Texas live oaks mostly, were small. But the sky was big. The sensation of light was dazzling, and the wide open spaces seemed somehow friendly and accessible, producing an atmosphere that was mercifully not too intimidating for a Temple, Texas, small-town boy with big-city aspirations.

I had seen SMU and a few other schools, of course, but they'd come across as a bit aloof, maybe a bit too *shady,* in fact. In contrast, TCU was warm, down-to-earth, and welcoming, if a bit yellow. Early on, though, I found myself thinking "what if"—what if TCU had sprinkler systems, ivy-clad walls, and beds of seasonal flowers? Looking back from today's verdant campus, it was as if I'd had a crystal ball, except for the ivy-covered walls. I'm still waiting for those.

As my dad and I unloaded his car, a big teal blue Buick Electra 225 with eight-track stereo, and my mom tried to put on a brave face since I was the first of three sons to leave home, we were surrounded by a bunch of "cool guys," all smiles and

Yearbook 1979, page 9. An aerial view of TCU campus shows various buildings such as Sadler Hall, Dave Reed Hall, the TCU Coliseum and Stadium, and several dorms.

confidence, with hearty handshakes. I didn't know it, but fraternity rush had already begun. I was instantly "snowed." Briefly distracted by one other group, I soon found myself and one of my two roommates in Milton Daniel, a.k.a. the "Milton Hilton," and pledged to Phi Kappa Sigma. Incidentally, the red and yellow scheme stopped inside Milton Daniel Hall, where the entire interior—walls, floors, and furniture—was brown.

Almost immediately, my TCU Quadrangle existence expanded to the brand-new Worth Hills Greek houses. The young oaks there were also struggling to provide shade, not to grassy lawns, but to asphalt. Even today, the unifying element of the fraternity and sorority houses is a less-than-beautiful parking lot. My crystal ball suggests that, like the huge lot that once greeted visitors to the old Quadrangle, green will eventually also prevail at Worth Hills.

Visual relief on the southwest side of the fraternity houses was provided by the duck pond and rolling hills beyond, which had been a municipal golf course until TCU's 106-acre purchase in 1961. I spent my sophomore, junior, and senior years in the Phi Kap house, two of those on the "green side" where big sky sunsets over the fallow hills were reflected in that placid little body of water. In spite of an inner shyness, I was a social animal on the outside and very involved. Consequently, the quiet side of my TCU home offered much needed respite, even solace, at times. I used to look out my window at the pink, orange, and (of course!) purple evening skies and think how lucky I was to be in the right place at the right time. My guess is that students today still find pleasure and comfort in that sweeping view, not of fallow hills, but of what has to be one of the finest and most beautiful athletic complexes in the

Yearbook 1979, page 9. Brown-Lupton Student Center glows in the dark as sunset disappears beyond the horizon. The Student Center provides the students with a place to gather, a place to study, or just a place to be yourself.

country. Alas, I'm getting ahead of myself.

Part of what makes TCU such a special place, a hundred years ago and today, is its topography and the way Fort Worth grew up around it. When the school first moved to the present campus, after a year in temporary lodgings downtown, it was three miles outside of the city proper. Imagine the vistas those early students enjoyed from the few

classical, columned buildings along the then-dirt road that was to become University Drive. Early aerial views illustrate just how country-like, how western, a setting it was. The flatlands along University provided a perfect setting for today's semi-circular classical layout crowned by Sadler Hall, the handsome remnants of a 1910 campus master plan.

RIGHT
Artist's rendering of remodeled Amon G. Carter Stadium provided by HKS Sports & Entertainment Group. In December 2010, the original Carter Stadium was demolished to make way for this auspicious addition to campus. The new stadium is expected to open in 2012.

BOTTOM RIGHT
Artist's rendering of remodeled football stadium provided by HKS Sports & Entertainment Group. After over fifty years in the current Amon G. Carter Stadium, TCU's nationally ranked football program needs room to grow.

Yearbook 1968, pages 10-11. Campus view.

With the exception of the original, elegant, alas, now-engulfed Mary Couts Burnett Library, most early campus development headed west, where flatland gives way to a gentle but substantial slope. Until recently, an all but mystical experience for those of us convinced that our blood is purple was to stand at the top of that slope on the plaza in front of the late, quintessentially 1950s Brown-Lupton Student Center as the sun set behind the monumental Amon G. Carter Stadium, the fiery West Texas sky tinting the falling water of Frog Fountain. You notice, I'm sure, how much sunsets figure into a lot of my TCU experience. While nostalgia for that prairie scene will no doubt remain with many alumni, the new Campus Commons, capped by Scharbauer Hall and

anchored by the magnificent, dramatically relocated Brown-Lupton University Union, provides an equally memorable experience, dense for sure, but in the best TCU tradition, bright and inviting.

The sense of place that makes TCU TCU is stronger now than ever. It's the same, only different from my rah-rah student days. And, if you need proof and a knock-out view, breathtaking in more ways than one, just climb to the upper deck of the beloved "Amon G." with its handsome and architecturally appropriate new Meyer-Martin Athletic Complex. Though that view will be altered with the stadium renovations, an equally impressive one will surely replace it. Look eastward toward the University Union, with its landmark clock tower and all of those red roofs and

Advertisements

Birdseye View of Fort Worth—Railroad, College and Industrial Center

We Patronize Those Whose "Ads" Are Found on the Following Pages

Yearbook 1915.
Start of the advertisement section.

now grand trees and the perfect spire of Robert Carr Chapel, an exact replica of that at the Old Lyme Church in Connecticut. From that lofty perspective, I challenge any alum to resist "memories sweet."

When I attend home football games, I am always struck by how *monumental* the stadium is. I was a cheerleader in my senior year, and in a reverse of most early memories when what once seemed grand becomes diminished with time, Amon G. Carter and the Moncrief Fields never cease to impress with their sheer scale and the audacity of that upper deck slope.

TCU is fortunate to be all but surrounded by gentle, leafy residential neighborhoods, some rather modest, others a bit grand, all enhancing its collegiate atmosphere. I hope that some McMansions, so invasive elsewhere, spare this lovely part of the world, which is also home to good neighbors such as the beloved and progressive Fort Worth Zoo and gracious Colonial Country Club. Of course, I never cut class to take a date to the zoo on a beautiful Friday afternoon in spring or fall!

Yearbook 1923, page 29.
Panorama of all buildings.

Looking at old photographs of the early campus, before there were any residential neighborhoods at all, I'm struck by how a classical revival aesthetic is returning to twenty-first century TCU, thanks to the vision and inspired leadership of the youngest looking and thinking chancellor in the country, Victor Boschini. He calls the new aesthetic "collegiate beaux arts," and his enthusiasm for it is contagious. To my eye, it is sort of "classical meets the twenty-first century." While I love great modern architecture and am proud of a number of modernist and contemporary buildings on campus, such as the Kevin Roche John Dinkeloo and Associates-designed Moudy building, the Tucker Technology Center, and its neighboring Smith Entrepreneurs Hall, and to a slightly lesser extent, Paul Rudolph's Sid Richardson Physical Sciences Building, like many I feared that TCU was in danger of losing its all-important cohesive *residential* personality. Too many architectural styles and, to my mind, some unfortunate additions, such as the library entrance that breaks what was once a clear axis from Sadler Hall to the Tandy Center, might have created a visual hodgepodge. Thanks to Dr. Boschini and the rest of today's TCU leadership, that fear has been put to rest. "Hail, all Hail," ladies and gentlemen.

The courtly campus architecture of old and the romantic landscapes and landmarks of another era, such as a bandstand and maypole that once stood in front of Jarvis Hall and a reflecting lily pond that graced the entrance of the original library, are appropriate inspirations not only for TCU's new collegiate beaux arts buildings, but also for important smaller landmarks. I find a sense of peace and pride sitting by Gayle's Pond in the Campus Commons. As a lucky veteran of the U.S. Army, I am struck by the simple dignity of the restored and enlarged Veterans Memorial Plaza along University Drive. The tablets there command my heartfelt reflection and respect. On the other hand, I get a kick out of sculptures such as *15 Cubes* in front of Smith Hall and the spiky, oddly charming Horned Frog between Sadler and Reed Halls with its plaque that reads simply, "to promote spirit and tradition."

In a sunny post-football game tour of the campus a few seasons ago, my brother and Horned Frog nephews watched students posing with the prominent statue of Messrs. Addison and Randolph Clark, arm-in-arm, purple and white pompons in all hands, flesh and bronze. We had to follow suit, and the results are little framed treasures. Just this fall, while showing off the Commons to an alumna friend from Dallas, we hammed it up for the camera, kissing that crazy, spiky frog. Large or small, campus landmarks are part of the TCU experience—positive and uplifting, especially in today's hard-edged and tense world.

While restoration and enhancement of old buildings such as Bailey and Jarvis are vital to TCU's sense of place and keep alumni feeling connected, the scope and grandeur of phenomenal new construction, particularly the Campus Commons, is a source of amazement and enormous pride. This is over the top, pure "wow" factor. I've walked the colonnades flanking the Commons at least a dozen times, and each time is like the first,

complete with an adrenaline rush and reassurance that this is a good place, that here anything is possible. Within that new territory, though, stands a long-time landmark that speaks to tradition, the highly visible, instantly recognizable Phillips, a.k.a. Frog, Fountain.

I'll never forget the origins of Frog Fountain. Decades after the late, lamented library reflecting pool had been overtaken by prosaic building expansion, not one fountain could be found on the campus in my senior year of 1969. Who wouldn't, therefore, have welcomed some watery relief from the Texas sun, not to mention a beautiful focal point for campus events? A small but very vocal group of students, that's who. War was raging in Vietnam, and students everywhere were questioning traditional values, even at TCU. I was, however, happy with tradition and thanking the Almighty that, at least at that point, I was safely ensconced in Worth Hills. Though the fountain was a gift from the H.H. Phillips family of San Antonio, controversy—ungrateful and short-sighted in my opinion—erupted over their generosity. Scholarships were the demanded alternatives.

While I often wonder how the protests made the family feel in 1969, I can only imagine how gratifying their gift ultimately was to them, not to mention to several generations of Horned Frogs since. Can you imagine TCU without it? While I felt nostalgia for the old mid-century Brown-Lupton and those wide open spaces of the Quadrangle, I am, like countless others, delighted that Frog Fountain has claimed its rightful place at the hub of campus life, with a larger, more beautiful pool base in addition.

No reflections on the TCU campus, then and now, would be complete or, indeed, appropriate without acknowledgment of the incredibly dedicated and generous individuals and families whose largesse has been key to all we take pride in today. The honor roll reads like a Who's Who of Fort Worth's first families, as well as prominent Texans all across the state and Texans, both honorary and native, beyond its borders. Not all can be listed in this limited space, but a walk through the old and new TCU reveals their names in stone and metal, carved not just into buildings and plaques, but also indelibly into the hearts of all who love this special place. One whose memory is reflected in flowers and all important greenery, rather than stone or bronze, is Mary Evans Beasley, whose 1987 endowment makes campus life more beautiful through each of the four seasons. Hats off to each one and thank you.

As I finish these random musings while visiting the campus in mid-December 2009, I've just come back inside Mary Couts Burnett Library after an outdoor break. It is almost dusk. There is an enormous and beautiful Christmas tree in the new Campus Commons, standing opposite Frog Fountain, decorated with silver and purple balls and white lights. The open arch of the University Union perfectly frames it on Stadium Drive. Sadler Hall and its stately columns are adorned with lights. The air is dry and cold, fragrant with freshly mown winter rye at the library entrance. The western sky that struck me on my first visit, a long time ago now, is still big, its scattered clouds gilded with yellow and silver, streaked with lavender and, yes, purple.

The TCU buff buildings are glowing in reflection, but there's no chance of mistaking yellow as our school color. We've just completed an undefeated football season, celebrated all over the nation, and the color purple is everywhere. A couple of weeks earlier, Fort Worth Mayor Mike

Moncrief even attempted to turn the Trinity River purple. If not as effective a dye job as in biblical days, the symbolism was impressive. As Fort Worth got behind TCU like never before, the mayor proclaimed the Trinity "Horned Frog River" for the duration of the year. I am happy to be a Horned Frog and to be back on campus. At the end of the day, Texas Christian University is not the same, only different from when I was enrolled. It is the same, only better.

....

MIKE MULLINS, *Class of 1969*

7

ONE HUNDRED YEARS OF TCU ATHLETICS

MARK MOURER

TCU football prepares for victory over Air Force, September 1998.

The nation was outraged over the manner in which college football's annual honors were bestowed. Criticism flowed from media members across the country over controversial post-season selection processes. Fans from coast to coast were incensed that some of the finest players and programs from outside the elite circles were being denied their opportunity to compete and be recognized on a national scale. A sportswriter for the *Mansfield News,* an Ohio newspaper, even wrote that some "sporting editors must be devoid of all sense of humor, judging by the way in which they permit their football writers to pick 'All-American' elevens."

That year was not 2003, when Auburn's unbeaten football team was denied its chance to play for a national championship, being cast aside by sportswriters, computer formulae, and pollsters.

The year was not 1974, when an undefeated Oklahoma Sooners squad shared the mythical national title, winning the Associated Press crown while a 10-1-1 Southern Cal team received the nod from the United Press. The year was 1910, and the college football world was furious over a mostly Ivy League All-American team. So furious were they, in fact, that they likely did not even notice that the Texas Christian University Horned Frogs played their first season in Fort Worth, finishing 2-6-1.

Flash forward a century from that 1910 season, and scandalous talk about players and teams getting snubbed has not diminished. However, the Horned Frogs capped one of their finest football campaigns since that two-win effort one hundred years ago. In 2010, TCU finished at number six in the final 2009 season polls with a 12-1 record,

RIGHT
Yearbook 1925, page 198.
Carlos Ashley, one of the best yell
leaders in the conference. Worked
very hard to support TCU teams.

BELOW
Yearbook 1938, page 186. "Lil"
Davey O'Brien. Thousands of words
have been written about the Frog's
No. 8...how can the Horned Frog tell
briefly of the exploits of this Dallas
Woodrow Wilson all-starter...it was
his kick that won the SMU game...
it was he who led the Frogs all
season..figures best show what Davey
meant to the Frogs..the Purple ran
730 plays (runs, passes, punts, field
goal attempts) in 1937...he was either
the ball carrier, the passer or the
kicker on 486 of these...he ran with
it 166 times for 533 yards gain, the
leading total...passed 234 times,
completing 96 for 947 yards, punted
83 times, and attempted 3 field goals,
making two...in addition returned 10
kick-offs for 273 yards and 63 punts
for 549 yards.

The Yell Leaders

CARLOS ASHLEY, one of the best yell leaders in the Conference, has given T. C. U. something that has been lacking in the past, and that thing is unified yelling. He has originated several new yells, which, together with the best of the old ones, has served to put the old school in the fore when it comes to real cheering. He has also trained four assistants in the gentle art of directing massed enthusiasm so as to get the best effects. Babe Haden, Chet Hagler, Ned Campbell, and Blubber Lovvorn are assistants who are really capable and who are all able individually to lead yells with the best of them.

They have all worked hard to get everyone out and interested in the teams, and they have succeeded largely because they have given so much of their energies to getting the full support of the students. Probably never before have we had such a corps of leaders who were respected so highly and who could command at every instant the best that was in the loyal supporters of the Purple and White warriors.

CARLOS ASHLEY

"BABE" HADEN

GIRLS' PEP SQUAD
Sheppard, Jennings, Taylor, Penn, Ellington, Haggard, Paine, White, Walton, Pratt, Hill.

completing an undefeated regular season. Their lone loss came only to Boise State in the Tostitos Fiesta Bowl—TCU's first Bowl Championship Series (BCS) appearance. Only the 1938 and 1935 squads, both of which earned national championship acclaim in the country's major poll systems, might make a better argument for the all-time TCU team. The 1935 squad featured Sam Baugh, one of the most lauded quarterbacks to play football at any level. The undefeated 1938 team saw Davey O'Brien win the coveted Heisman Trophy.

Horned Frog Football, including Jim Swink's 1955 Southwest Conference champions and LaDainian Tomlinson's 406 yards against UTEP that broke the single-game rushing record on November 20, 1999, has been memorable, but most college football pundits would agree that the 2009 team was the finest TCU gridiron squad in several generations. However, hardly anyone— from media expert to casual tailgater—could experience the season without dwelling at least partially on some of its controversy.

Gary Patterson came to TCU in 1998 as its defensive coordinator under former head coach Dennis Franchione, and they began a winning tradition that is unrivaled in TCU athletic history. With due respect to national championship-winning coach L.D. "Dutch" Meyer and legendary Abe Martin after him, TCU has only suffered one losing season in the twelve that have followed "Coach Fran's" arrival. The Tomlinson-led Frogs were the first non-BCS team to threaten the BCS monopoly in 2000, but lost to San Jose State. Patterson took over as head coach when Franchione left for the same position at the University of Alabama, and he narrowly lost his first game as head coach in the 2000 GMAC Mobile Bowl. Patterson's Frogs knocked on the BCS door again in 2003, only to lose to Southern Mississippi on the last game of the regular season. Between 1998, when TCU shocked Southern Cal in the Northwest Sun Bowl, and the Glendale, Arizona, trip in 2010, TCU played in a bowl game after every season except 2004.

If anything ran congruent throughout the last one hundred years in college football, it is that each season remains sprinkled with debate, dissension, and disunion among final rankings. Fortunately, the other twenty sports that have had National Collegiate Athletic Association (NCAA) representation from Horned Frogs have not been as riddled with brewing storms.

Perhaps no TCU teams have been as consistent in winning as the women's basketball teams, coached by Jeff Mittie since 1999. Owning an impressive 216-106 record, Mittie has won over

ABOVE
Yearbook 1995, page 302.
1995 football team.

ABOVE (LOWER)
Yearbook 1938, page 174.
1937 Horned Frog Squad.
53 members in all.

ABOVE RIGHT
Yearbook 1959, page 72.
The Horned Frogs wait for
the half time activities to
be over.

half of the Lady Frogs' all-time games. TCU women's basketball existed as a club sport throughout the mid-twentieth century, but did not begin NCAA play until 1977, entering Division I in 1982. However, its 424 all-time wins did not include a post-season victory until Head Coach Mike Peterson's final season with TCU, when his Lady Frogs beat UTEP 67-58 in the first round of the Western Athletic Conference (WAC) Tournament in Las Vegas. Since then, Mittie's teams have gone to the NCAA Tournament eight times beginning in 2001, with the lone non-invitation year coming in 2008, when they made it to the quarterfinals of the Women's NIT in Boulder.

Judy Daley began coaching the Lady Frogs in 1977 and notched the program's first win against Navarro Junior College. Kenneth Davis was the coach to guide the women's cagers into Southwest Conference and Division I play before Fran Garmon took over in 1983. Coach Garmon recruited Janice Dziuk from Poth, Texas, and Dziuk's 1,448 career points would stand as the team record from her senior season in 1990 until All-American Sandora Irvin's 1,892 eclipsed her mark fifteen years later. Adrianne Ross has since climbed into second place with 1,725, earning that position in 2008. Irvin also leads in all-time rebounding with 1,370 grabs during her career, and was drafted into the WNBA.

TCU baseball teams have won several conference championships throughout numerous affiliations with the Southwest Conference (SWC),

The first year of the modern varsity women's basketball team, 1974-1975. Photo courtesy of Bob Frye.

Lance Broadway, who were drafted into professional organizations following their careers on the TCU diamond.

One of the most decorated programs to don TCU's purple has been both men's and women's track and field. Horned Frogs began competing in 1923 and have claimed numerous national championships beginning in 1983, when Allen Ingraham, James Richard, Keith Burnett, and David Walker won the 4 X 400 meter relay at the NCAA Outdoor Championships in Houston. Foreshadowing years of relay dominance, the "Flyin' Frogs'" first 4 X 100 relay championship came in 1986, when Roscoe Tatum, Andrew Smith, Leroy Reid, and Greg Sholars brought home the title for Head Coach Bubba Thornton. They repeated in 1987, with future Olympian Raymond Stewart anchoring Tatum, Smith, and Sholars' quarter-mile effort.

Stewart still holds the school record for the 100-meter dash at 9.89 seconds, won silver at the 1988 Olympics, and brought home two national championships in the 100-meter in 1987 and 1989. He is among a solid recruiting pipeline of accomplished sprinters and relay team members from Jamaica, including Smith, seven-time All-American Michael Frater, and former Olympian Beverly McDonald, who earned a silver medal in the 2000 games.

Former Head Coach Monte Stratton and current coach Darryl Anderson have continued to produce fantastic finishers, including Olympic Gold Medalist Jon Drummond, who was on the 2000 4 X 100 team that won it all in Sydney. In 2003, World Track and Field Champion Kim Collins claimed his gold in the 100-meter final. Additional NCAA championships were won by Horatio Porter, Smith, Sholars, and Stewart in 1989, and Porter was joined by Drummond,

Conference USA, and the Mountain West Conference (MWC). Former Head Coach Frank Windegger, who also served as TCU's Athletic Director from 1974 until 1997, coached four SWC Championship teams (1963, '66, '67 and '72) and three SWC runner-up squads. Current Head Coach Jim Schlossnagle has won the Mountain West Conference Championship each of the four years the Horned Frogs have competed in the conference, having also won the last two Conference USA Tournaments prior to switching leagues. Schlossnagle will take a 251-120 (.677) TCU record into the 2010 season. Former Frogs include previous Head Coach and Houston Astro Lance Brown, former Major League All-Star Jeff Zimmerman, and dozens of other players like Jim Busby and

Yearbook 1968, page 316. The weather clinched the SWC baseball crown for UT this spring. TCU finished second by a few percentage points after rain cancelled their late season double-header with A&M and a new rule barred replays of games postponed in the last half of the season. Ironically, TCU baseball coach Frank Windegger had predicted that the new rule could cause trouble. The Frog baseballers, however, had a good season, if a frustrating one. Their 13-5 record left them with .722 behind the Longhorn's .750.

Carey Johnson, and Ralston Wright to win the national championship in the 4 X 100 relay in 1991. Donovan Powell, Khadevis Robinson, Roy Williams, Syan Williams, Johnny Collins, and Jackson Langat all won national championships while running for the Frogs. Joe Brown won the Mountain West Athlete of the Year in 2008 while throwing the javelin for TCU, and, along with four-time All-American long jumper Aundre Edwards, stands among several field specialists who competed for TCU.

Virgil Hodge is perhaps one of the most decorated women to run for TCU's track and field teams, representing her native St. Kitts in the 2008 Olympics. All-Americans Dywana Crudup, Donita Harmon, and Tinesha Jackson-Hackney join Monica Twum, Deborah Jones, Nathandra John, and Donna Thomas as women track stars who won conference titles and placed nationally at NCAA meets.

Just before the move to Fort Worth, TCU began fielding men's basketball teams, but did not play consistently until the 1913-14 season. As the Horned Frogs shot their way into the twenties, they started getting some consistent winning play before Francis Schmidt began winning Southwest Conference titles in the 1930s. The first TCU Men's Basketball All-American, Ad Dietzel, took the court in 1931, followed by Wallace Myers in 1933.

The men's cagers never threatened in the SWC until Buster Brannon took over in 1948. The

RIGHT
Yearbook 1924, page 223.
The sophomore hockey team
(field hockey) (female).
From L to R: Winnie Williams,
Ruth Seymour, Ethel Harkins,
Mrs. Donaldson, Frances Wilson,
Ripple Sweet, Dorothy LeMond,
Emilie Stubbs, Cora Mae Tadlock,
Empress Gough, and Mabel Mills.

LOWER RIGHT
Yearbook 1961, page 309.
Reagan Gassaway just couldn't
catch the SMU speedster in
the baton event.

Frogs won a share of the conference in Brannon's third season, going 16-9 overall and winning the conference outright three more times in the 1950s. George McLeod, H. E. Kirchner, and Dick O'Neal all garnered All-American honors for Brannon while advancing to the NCAA Regional Tournament in 1952, '53 and '59—the years they won the SWC titles. O'Neal still ranks fourth in all-time points scored with 1,723, and maintains a share of the TCU title for points per game average at 23.9. Moreover, long before he became the first tenured African American professor in Harvard's School of Business, James Cash earned the first Southwest Conference scholarship for an

Yearbook 1934, page 113. Charlie Casper. He has been a record-breaking track man for seven years of competition. At TCU he has set a new all-time scoring record his junior year and has won every hurdle race he has participated in in the Southwest Conference. As a high school participant Casper went to Chicago and set a new world record in the high hurdles his senior year. The time was 15.1 seconds.

African American when he came to TCU in 1966. Head Coach Johnny Swaim took over the court in 1968. He inherited two-time conference first teamer Mickey McCarty, generally regarded as one of the finest all-around athletes to ever play in the SWC. McCarty averaged a double-double his senior season when the Frogs went to Swaim's first of two NCAA Regionals (18.8 points per game and 11.8 rebounds per game) before being drafted by two professional basketball organizations, one pro football outfit, and a major league baseball team. Cash also lent a hand in that title, averaging 13.8 points per game and was also an Academic All-American for the first of two seasons in '68. Even though he was only at TCU for one season, he made it a memorable one, when Eugene "Goo" Kennedy helped lead the '71 squad back to regionals and nabbed the SWC crown. Kennedy still holds the record for field goal percentage for that '71 season (212-360 / .589) and for single-season rebounds per game with 16.6—almost four more per game than second place Ronny Stevenson.

Mirroring the football Frogs' futility in the seventies, the men's hoops squad went 45-136 throughout the rest of the decade. Jim Killingsworth took over in 1980, earning a share of the conference title in the 1985-86 season and an outright crown in 1987. The Frogs' last NCAA Regional Tournament appearance came in 1998, when Head Coach Billy Tubbs and future National Basketball Association (NBA) draftee Lee Nailon lost to Florida State in the first round. Neil Dougherty's Horned Frogs lasted three games into the National Intercollegiate Tournament (NIT) in 2005, and Jim Christian took over the court for the Frogs in 2008. Coaching changes can be commonplace among collegiate athletics, but TCU has been fortunate to have several coaches commit to the lives of their student-athletes for several years.

One of the longest-tenured head coaches in TCU history is Richard Sybesma, handling both men's and women's swimming and diving programs. Swimming was a club sport when Sybesma arrived in 1978, and his men's team won the Mountain West Conference title in 2010. He's won Coach of the Year several times in multiple conferences and coached the Nicaraguan Olympic team in 1996. A former captain of the Texas Tech swim team, Sybesma's greatest contributions to TCU athletics are his numerous All-American Scholar titles (thirty-four for women swimmers, twelve for men swimmers) and the departmental cumulative GPA, which has been near 3.0 for over ten years. TCU has had twelve women's All-American swimmers and two men's All-Americans under Sybesma's watch.

TCU Women's Golf took the 1983 National Championship under Head Coach Fred Warren, beating Tulsa after having finished second to the Golden Hurricane the year before. That '83 team also won women's golf's first and only SWC title. Rita Moore, Anne Kelly, Marci Bozarth, Rae

ABOVE
Yearbook 1961, page 289. Keeping an eye on both the mid-court stripe and an Austin defender. Don Rosick is wondering how to evade both. Rosick hit four goals and made one at the free-throw line for nine points.

ABOVE RIGHT
Yearbook 1978, page 169. Tim Marion launches a high flier over a bear.

LOWER RIGHT
Yearbook 1979, page 111. Fighting Frogs on the Court: TCU's 1978-79 basketball team.

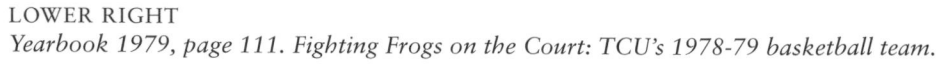

Yearbook 1965, page 178. Some of the golf winners are pictured L to R: Susan Anderson, Carol Williams, PBP; Nancy Hickcock, DDD; Susan Swindle, KAT; Debbie Hargrove, DG; and Karen McMillian, ZTA.

Rothfelder, and Jenny Lidback won the national title at the Georgia Golf Club in Athens. "The key is that we got off to a good start," Warren said about the tournament. "I thought we could shoot this course under par, but we always got off to such a bad start we were always just trying to get back to par the first three days. But I had a good feeling coming out here today. I just really thought we would win, and it's much more satisfying to do it by beating an excellent Tulsa team."

Another coach nearing her second decade at the helm of a Horned Frog program is women's golf coach Angie Ravaioli-Larkin. A former collegiate golfer herself, "Coach Angie" began her tenure during the closing years of the Southwest Conference. She won titles in each of the following conference stops, beginning with the Western Athletic Conference title in 1997-98. The women's

golfers did so again in 2001-02, winning the Conference USA crown. After each conference title, Larkin's squads finished runner-up three consecutive years in both conferences, marking an incredible run as conference numbers one or two for eight consecutive years. They would take the Mountain West title in 2006-07. Seven All-Americans have played women's golf for TCU, including current Ladies Professional Golf Association (LPGA) touring pro Angela Stanford.

Like the women's golf team, TCU's men's duffers have also won conference titles in all four conferences of competition. First claiming their SWC title in 1986, the team had two All-Americans in Jim Sorenson and Pete Jordan, under Head Coach Bill Woodley. Bill Montigel took over after Woodley left for the University of Arkansas. Montigel, a former assistant basketball coach under

ABOVE
Yearbook 1965, page 179.
Archery winners are pictured left
to right: Sue Porter, Clods;
Ginny Liles, ZTA; Marsha
Barbour, Clods; Betsy McGraw,
DDD; and Martha Walls, Clods.

ABOVE RIGHT
Yearbook 1930, page 181.
Women's Riding Team. Many girls
joined the riding division of the
Texas Outing Club although they
did not attempt to make the full
thirty hours necessary for the
W.A.A. credit in the sport. Miss
Helen Jenkins was manager of this
sport. The girls rode at Tucker's
stables and at the cavalry camp at
least once a week.

Killingsworth, has coached at TCU for over twenty years. He coached a pair of WAC Championship teams in 1997 and again in 1998. Those two teams featured current Professional Golf Association (PGA) Touring Pro J.J. Henry, who finished tied for runner-up in the '98 NCAA National Championships in Auburn, Alabama. Montigel's teams won Conference USA titles for five consecutive years beginning in 2001, when another Horned Frog—this time Adam Rubinson—finished tied for second in 2002. Dan Jenkins, best-selling novelist and acclaimed writer for *Sports Illustrated, Golf Digest,* and others, captained the golf teams before he graduated in 1953, and paved the way for Don Massengale and Charles Coody to carry the torch for TCU Men's Golf through the sixties. Coody won the 1971 Masters in Augusta, Georgia.

TCU tennis squads have also proudly been led by long-tenured head coaches throughout their proud histories and have had numerous All-Amer-

icans between the men's and women's teams. Beginning with the first All-American netter in Randy Crawford in 1977, David Pate and Karl Richter, also All-Americans, claimed the NCAA doubles championship in 1981 when the men's team flourished under long-time Head Coach "Tut" Bartzen. Esteban Carril, David Pate, and Paul Robinson were named All-American in singles for three years while competing for the Frogs.

Roland Ingram began coaching the women's team in 1983 and won four conference titles in nineteen seasons. Ingram's women's tennis teams won the SWC Championship in 1991, WAC Championships in 2000 and 2001, and a Conference USA Championship in 2002. Dave Borelli took over and won the first of three consecutive Mountain West regular season championships in 2006 before taking over the men's team. When Jefferson Hammond arrived, he continued the winning ways in the MWC, taking either the regular season or conference tournament champi-

Yearbook 1971, page 185. Marksmen. Several activities on campus go unnoticed by almost everyone. Unfortunately, due to the lack of space and many other difficulties, these activities seldom receive complete coverage in the yearbook.

onships the next three years. Nine women's tennis players have earned All-America honors during TCU's net play, which began in 1972.

TCU women's soccer has only known two head coaches since the team began competitive play in 1986. Guiding both men's and women's soccer squads, David Rubinson handled coaching detail for nineteen years, winning Coach of the Year honors in 1997. Eventually, women's soccer became a scholarship-funded sport in the early twenty-first century, and the men's team was disbanded. Prior to that, all participants had been walk-ons. Current Head Coach Dan Abdalla took over in 2005, leading the team to its all-time best record of 14-4-2 in 2008. Lizzy Karoly finished her career in 2010 as women's soccer's all-time leading scorer.

The newest programs to compete for TCU have been the rifle teams, volleyball squads, and equestrian riders. Prentice Lewis assumed head coaching duties for the TCU Women's Volleyball team in 2002, six years after the program began play under first Head Coach Sandy Troudt. The 2009 squad recorded the best finish in the fifteen-year history of the program, finishing at 27-7 for Prentice Lewis' fifth twenty-win season as a head coach. Moreover, the '09 squad earned their first NCAA Tournament appearance, advancing to the second round after beating Rice.

TCU's Equestrian Team wasted no time in making their mark on the national competitive landscape, winning the first team national championship for the 2007-08 season. It was only the second historic first for the program, however, as the team had advanced to the national championships in its first year of competition the previous season. Head Coach Gary Reynolds handles both English and Western equestrian riding.

And, finally, as the one hundredth anniver-

sary of athletic competition for Horned Frogs in Fort Worth comes to pass, the 2010 women's rifle team closes out its season as national champions. Ironically, with Fort Worth's "Hell's Half Acre" gunfights, saloons, brothels, and gambling houses, TCU's women's marksmen bring home the latest NCAA crown for TCU Athletics. Far different than the gunslinging pistol work made famous by Jim Courtright and Bat Masterson, the Horned Frog rifle teams used smallbore and air rifles to achieve their success. Sweeter still is the host site for the 2010 National Championship: TCU's own Daniel-Meyer Coliseum.

Karen Monez, head coach for the women's team, won the 2007 National Rifle Association

Yearbook 1938, page 181. The Purple defended its goal line perfectly against the Mustangs, but Frog supporters held their breath as this pass fell incomplete. Davey O'Brien was just too short to stop it, and SMU's Pete Acker is hopefully watching the ball. At the right are SMU's Jackson and the Frogs' Ki Aldrich. In the background can be seen part of the crowd that filled the stadium that day.

ABOVE
*Yearbook 1986, page 138.
The cheerleaders proudly
raise spirit during the Homecoming Pep Rally.*

ABOVE (CENTER)
*Yearbook 1965, page 3.
Inside cover page.*

ABOVE (FAR RIGHT)
*Yearbook 1990, page 4.
Super Frog.*

Distinguished College Coach of the Year Award. She had coached four All-Americans in her six seasons at the helm of the program, and Monez's teams had placed no lower than fifth in aggregate scoring for smallbore and air rifle competition prior to the 2010 crown. The 2010 team named five additional All-Americans to the squad, including Erin Lorenzen, Sarah Scherer, Sarah Beard, Simone Riford, and Caitlin Morrissey.

TCU's second century in athletic competition, with Fort Worth as its hometown, will begin in August 2010. Hopes are high for the football team, fresh off its first BCS Championship and returning sixteen starters. Women's soccer will continue to build toward an NCAA tournament appearance, while women's volleyball will aim to build on their first tournament appearance. Mittie's women's basketball squad, having earned a ninth NCAA Tournament appearance in 2010, will hope to progress toward the Sweet 16, as the men's team under Jim Christian will hope to build back to the successes known under Killingsworth, Swaim, and Tubbs. There are outstanding opportunities for more conference—and even national—championships for all Horned Frog sports for the next one hundred years.

MARK MOURER
Assistant Dean, College of Communication

ABOUT THE CONTRIBUTORS

VICKI VINSON CANTWELL

Cantwell is a Fort Worth civic leader and museum collection management advisor who has worked with such prestigious institutions as the Victoria and Albert Museum in London, the J. Paul Getty Museum in Los Angeles, and the Modern Art Museum in Fort Worth. She earned her BA in art history from TCU and her MA from SMU. She was named TCU's Valuable Alumna in 2007 and currently serves on the board of directors of Humanities Texas.

BOB J. FRYE

Emeritus professor of English Bob J. Frye is in his forty-fifth year of teaching at Texas Christian University, where he has been a Cecil and Ida Green Distinguished Emeritus Tutor in English. He received the Chancellor's Award for Distinguished Teaching in 1992, was named a Piper Professor of Texas in 1994 by the Minnie Stevens Piper Foundation of San Antonio, and in 1996 was selected Texas Professor of the Year by the Carnegie Foundation for the Advancement of Teaching.

He earned his PhD from the University of Tennessee, has published two books and many articles and reviews, and served as the first TCU women's varsity basketball coach in 1974-75. He was named an Honorary TCU Alumnus in 2008.

MARK MOURER

Mourer served as a reporter and campus editor for the *TCU Daily Skiff* and graduated from TCU with a BS in journalism. He also holds an MS from TCU. He has been involved with media relations, interning for KXAS NBC 5 and also serving as public relations coordinator at the Texas Motor Speedway. He has been affiliated with the TCU Frog Club, and he now works in medical sales for Mead Johnson Nutritionals and teaches part-time at TCU.

MICHAEL MULLINS

Mullins graduated from TCU with a degree in history and, after serving in the U.S. Army, spent his early career years in New York City, where he graduated from the American Academy of Dramatic Arts. Most notably, he worked on *The Dick Cavett Show*. A video and live events producer, he spent twenty-one years in public relations and advertising with the Dallas Market Center Company. He produced the annual Dallas Fashion Awards and ARTS Awards for over a decade and is currently a producer of the International Folk Art Market in Santa Fe, New Mexico.

GENE ALLEN SMITH

Smith is director of The Center for Texas Studies at TCU, professor of history, and curator of history for the Fort Worth Museum of Science and History. He earned his PhD from Auburn University and has published seven books. Although not a native Texan, he adopted the state when he came to TCU in 1994.

RON TYLER

Former director of the Amon Carter Museum, Tyler was previously professor of history at the University of Texas and director of the Texas State Historical Association. He earned his PhD in history from TCU and has published more than two dozen books. He also serves on a number of foundations and other boards.

MARY L. VOLCANSEK

Volcansek is executive director of The Center for Texas Studies at TCU and professor of political science. A native Texan, she returned to Texas in 2000 to assume the deanship of TCU's AddRan College of Humanities and Social Sciences. Previously, she was professor of political science at Florida International University. She is author or editor of eleven books and serves on the board of Humanities Texas.

ACKNOWLEDGMENTS

This book would not have been possible without the generous support of the Lowe Foundation and the cheerful and informative faculty, alumni, and friends who contributed essays. I also wish to acknowledge the contributions of Amber Surmiller and Evan Vaughan, who tirelessly perused thousands of TCU photographs and yearbooks to find the right pictures to capture one hundred years of the Fort Worth and TCU partnership. Unless otherwise specified, all photographs are courtesy of TCU Library Special Collections. I also wish to thank the Burnett Foundation, the Amon G. Carter Foundation, the Jane and John Justin Foundation, the Lowe Foundation, the Summerlee Foundation, and the Summerfield G. Roberts Foundation, all of which have contributed to the operations of The Center for Texas Studies.

INDEX